D0955738

STOLEN INTO SLAVERY

STOLEN INTO SLAVERY

THE TRUE STORY OF SOLOMON NORTHUP, FREE BLACK MAN

BY JUDITH FRADIN AND DENNIS FRADIN

NATIONAL GEOGRAPHIC

WASHINGTON, D.C.

>»⟩⟩≕⟨⟨⟨«

With gratitude to Renee Moore, the founder of Solomon Northup Day, who was a tireless resource for us. We also thank the photo archivists at the Alexandria and Baton Rouge campuses of Louisiana State University for their gracious assistance, and the family of Sue Eakin, Solomon Northup biographer extraordinaire.
For the Louisiana branch of the Fradin family—Diana Judith, Michael James, Shalom Amelia, and Dahlia Sol Richard

Dust jacket design by Eva Absher and David M. Seager
Book design by David M. Seager
Text is set in Proforma Book. Display type is Ashwood and Hawksmoor.

Library of Congress Cataloging-in-Publication Data

Fradin, Judith Bloom.
Stolen into slavery : the true story of Solomon Northup, free black man / by Judy and Dennis Fradin.
p. cm.
Includes bibliographical references and index.
ISBN 978-1-4263-0937-3 (hardcover : alk. paper) -- ISBN 978-1-4263-0938-0 (library binding : alk. paper)
1. Northup, Solomon, b. 1808. 2. Slaves--United States--Biography. 3. African Americans--Biography. 4. Plantation life--Louisiana--History--19th century. 5. Slavery--Louisiana--History--19th century. I. Fradin, Dennis B. II. Title.
E444.N87F73 2012
306.3'62092--dc23
[B]
2011024664

Printed in the United States of America
11/QGT-LPH/1

NOTE FROM THE AUTHORS

WE FRADINS HAVE WRITTEN DOZENS OF BOOKS together. Researching and writing about the life of Solomon Northup has been both fascinating and inspiring.

Following the Civil War, many slaves wrote about their experiences. Solomon Northup's narrative, written prior to the Civil War, is particularly gripping. Having previously lived as a free man in New York State, his enslavement seemed all the more bitter. His desire to escape fueled his determination to survive. Solomon drew strength and solace from his music, which allowed him a temporary refuge from his seemingly endless years in Louisiana cane and cotton fields.

Soon after he returned to his wife and family, Northup published his autobiography, *Twelve Years a Slave.* That book was the source of much of the detail and all of the dialogue in *Stolen Into Slavery.* Solomon Northup's memoir, co-authored with David Wilson, reflects not only Northup's memory of his experiences but also his deepest feelings about them.

Of course, memory can be tricky. Therefore we verified the basic events of Solomon's life in bills of sale and in court records. But it is Solomon's interpretation of events that gives us a unique glimpse into that most "peculiar institution," American slavery.

—Judith and Dennis Fradin

CONTENTS

"WELL, MY BOY, HOW DO YOU FEEL NOW?"

SOLOMON NORTHUP AWOKE IN THE MIDDLE OF AN April night in 1841 with his body trembling, his head throbbing, and a terrifying question in his mind: Where was he? He slowly realized that he was in a dark, dank, foul-smelling dungeon in Washington, D.C. Worse yet, he was in handcuffs and his feet were chained to the floor.

As his head cleared, Solomon managed to slip a hand into his trousers pocket, where he had placed his money and his "free papers" for safekeeping. They were gone! He checked his other pockets and found no trace of the money or the papers that proved he was one of 400,000 "free blacks" in a nation where 2.5 million African Americans were slaves.

"There must have been some mistake," Solomon told himself. Any second now the two white men he had been traveling with would arrive to free him. But as the night wore on, he began to wonder whether these seemingly friendly men could have betrayed him.

The rising sun revealed that Solomon was in a cell with only one small window covered by thick iron bars. Soon he heard footsteps coming down the stairs. A key turned in a lock, the heavy iron door swung open, and two men entered the room where Solomon was chained.

"Well, my boy, how do you feel now?" asked one of the men, who Solomon later learned was named James Birch.

Solomon, who was 32 years old, wasn't accustomed to being called "boy," which was a demeaning way of addressing male slaves regardless of age. "What is the cause of my imprisonment?" Solomon demanded.

"I have bought you, and you are my slave," said Birch, adding that he planned to send him far south to New Orleans to be sold.

"I am a free man, a resident of Saratoga Springs, New York, where I have a wife and children who are also free, and my name is Northup!" Solomon protested. Furthermore, he vowed, once he was liberated from this hellhole he would prosecute Birch for kidnapping.

Birch was enraged. He called Solomon a "black liar" and insisted that he was a runaway slave from Georgia. As Solomon continued to assert that he was a free black man from New York, Birch ordered his assistant to bring him his paddle and whip. Ripping off Solomon's shirt, the assistant stood on his chains to pin him to the floor while Birch beat him with the paddle. From time to time Birch paused to ask whether Solomon still claimed that he had been free. Despite the intense pain, Solomon refused to say that he was a slave.

When the paddle broke, Birch picked up his whip. Soon streams of blood were pouring down Solomon's back, and strips of skin were gouged out wherever the lash struck. Even so, Solomon still wouldn't say what Birch demanded—that he was a fugitive slave from Georgia.

After a quarter of an hour Solomon was barely conscious and Birch's right arm was exhausted. As he put down his whip, Birch warned Solomon, "If you ever utter again that you are entitled to your freedom or that you have been kidnapped, the punishment you have just received is nothing compared with what will follow!" Birch and his assistant then departed, slamming the big iron door behind them.

Paddling was one of many methods used by owners to humiliate and control their slaves. This scene is set in the West Indies, but Solomon Northup suffered the same punishment in Washington, D.C.

Solomon had been beaten so savagely that for a few days he expected to die. His handcuffs and leg chains were removed but the pain from his injuries made movement difficult. His only contact with the outside world came twice a day when the assistant brought him a tin plate containing a piece of fried pork, a slice of bread, and a cup of water.

When he had healed enough to walk, he was allowed to

This slave pen is similar to the one in which Solomon Northup was held. Each door led to a dark, airless cell.

exercise in the yard with several other black prisoners in the building. One man whom he befriended, Clemens Ray, informed him that they were in a "slave pen"—a kind of prison where James Birch held his slaves before sending them down to New Orleans to be sold. The slave pen was so close to the U.S. Capitol that Solomon could see the building's dome from the yard.

Heartsick and furious about being enslaved, Solomon enjoyed peace of mind only when he went to sleep at night. Then he would dream that he was back in Saratoga Springs with his wife and their three children. But he always awakened to the realization that he was imprisoned in a jail cell in Washington, D.C., and, in the darkness, he would weep bitter tears.

Yet he did have one hope: escape! Fleeing from the slave pen was pretty much out of the question because the building was like a fortress and was surrounded by a tall, brick wall. But perhaps the trip to New Orleans would offer an opportunity to break free from this nightmare.

CHAPTER 2

"I WISHED FOR WINGS"

ALL 13 AMERICAN COLONIES ALLOWED SLAVERY DURING
the 1600s and 1700s. Not until 1780—four years after
the colonies declared themselves to be the United
States of America—did Pennsylvania become the first
state to outlaw slavery. Other northern states also made slavery
illegal, but some took their time doing so. Solomon Northup's
home state, New York, didn't outlaw slavery until 1827.

The black mother's status determined that of her children
in the slave states. If the mother was a slave, her children were,
too. If the mother was a free black, so were her children.

Solomon Northup was born in Minerva, New York, 100
miles south of the Canadian border and 200 miles north of
New York City. Solomon claimed that he had entered the world
"in the month of July, 1808." Since Solomon's mother was a free
black woman, he was born free.

On his father's side, Solomon's ancestors had been slaves
belonging to a white family named Northup. Around the year
1800 Solomon's father, Mintus, had been freed by the terms of
his owner's will. Mintus had adopted the last name Northup to
honor the family that had liberated him.

Solomon was a serious, hardworking child. When he
wasn't helping around the family farm, he loved to read. His
favorite pastime, however, was playing the violin. By his teens
Solomon was so skillful a fiddler that friends and neighbors
hired him to perform at dances and parties.

On Christmas Day of 1829, 21-year-old Solomon Northup
married Anne Hampton. Solomon liked to say that the blood

of three races flowed through Anne's veins: Native American, white, and black. The couple had three children—daughters Elizabeth and Margaret and a son, Alonzo.

In the spring of 1834 Solomon and his family settled in Saratoga Springs, a vacation resort 30 miles from Albany, the capital of New York. During the warm months when tourists flocked to Saratoga Springs to bathe in its mineral spring waters, Solomon drove a carriage for the hotels. At other times he worked as a carpenter, helping to build area railroads. In addition, Solomon earned an income from playing his violin. Meanwhile, Anne found employment as a cook in hotels and inns. By pinching pennies, Solomon and Anne managed to squeak by financially. Around Saratoga Springs, the Northups had a reputation for being a close and loving family.

One morning in late March of 1841 Solomon went for a walk in hope of finding an odd job. At the time, Anne was 20 miles away working as a cook at Sherrill's Coffee House in Sandy Hill, now known as Hudson Falls, for a few weeks. Anne had taken nine-year-old Elizabeth with her. Seven-year-old Margaret and five-year-old Alonzo were being cared for by an aunt in or near Saratoga Springs.

At the corner of Congress and Broadway, Solomon spied an acquaintance of his talking to two white strangers. "Solomon is an expert player on the violin," his acquaintance explained, while introducing him to the two men. The strangers, who said their names were Merrill Brown and Abram Hamilton, claimed to be in need of a violinist. They were headed to Washington, D.C., to meet the circus they worked for—or so they said—and a violinist would attract customers to the

Before he was kidnapped into slavery, Solomon drove a carriage like those waiting in front of the United States Hotel in Saratoga Springs, New York, in this early 20th-century photo.

small shows they would present along the way. Brown and Hamilton offered to pay Solomon a dollar a day for driving them in their carriage as far as New York City, plus three dollars for each performance and enough money for his return to Saratoga Springs.

Excited by the prospect of a windfall, Solomon hurried home and grabbed a suitcase, a few clothes, and his violin. Since he expected to be back home before Anne's return, he didn't even stop to leave his wife a note about where he was going. Solomon climbed into the driver's seat of Brown and Hamilton's carriage and drove away from Saratoga Springs as happy as he had ever been in his life.

Thirty miles into their journey, they stopped to present a show in Albany. Hamilton sold the tickets, Solomon provided violin music, and Brown amused the audience by juggling balls, walking on a tightrope, and making invisible pigs squeal. This proved to be their only performance en route to New York City, for Brown and Hamilton said they were worried that they wouldn't reach Washington in time to join up with the main body of the circus.

Once in New York City Solomon expected to be paid and then return home to Saratoga Springs. However, Brown and Hamilton had another exciting proposal. They promised that if Solomon continued with them to Washington, D.C., the circus would hire him for a more permanent job. Touring with the big show for a few weeks, he would earn more money than he made in an entire year in Saratoga Springs.

Solomon accepted the offer. His family could use the money. Besides, he trusted Brown and Hamilton, who seemed to be concerned for his welfare. For example, before leaving New York City they took Solomon to a government office to obtain free papers for him. That way if someone in Washington claimed he was a slave, Solomon could present written proof that he was free. This was important because slavery was legal in Washington, D.C. Any black person in our nation's capital risked being mistaken for a slave.

When they reached Baltimore, Maryland, Solomon

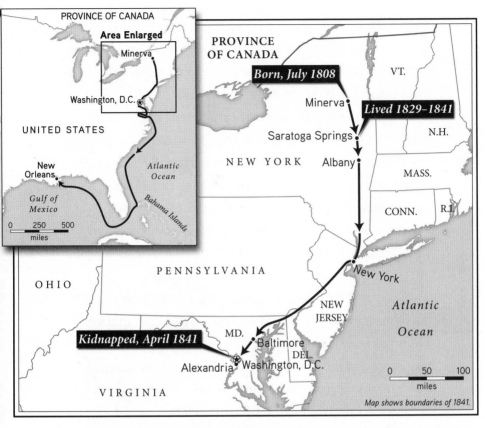

Solomon Northup spent the first 32 years of his life a free man in upstate New York. He was then lured to Washington, D.C., where he was sold into slavery.

parked the carriage. He and his two new friends boarded a train. With his free papers securely in his pocket, Solomon arrived in the U.S. capital with Brown and Hamilton on April 6, 1841. They checked in at Gadsby's, the city's top hotel, on Pennsylvania Avenue down the street from the White House.

Solomon and his companions arrived in the national

capital at a time of mourning. Two days earlier President William Henry Harrison had died in the White House after being in office for only 30 days, making Vice President John Tyler the new President. After supper Brown and Hamilton invited Solomon to their room, where they counted out $43 and handed it to him. That was more than he was due, but the two circus men insisted that he take a few extra dollars because it wasn't his fault that they had presented fewer performances than expected on the way to Washington. They invited Solomon to attend President Harrison's funeral procession with them the next day. Afterward, they promised, they would introduce Solomon to the circus company owners.

The next day, April 7, a giant funeral honoring the late President was held in Washington. Bells were tolled, cannons were fired, and thousands of people joined the procession on foot and in carriages. Several times during the ceremony Brown and Hamilton invited Solomon to join them for drinks in a nearby saloon. Unaccustomed to liquor, Solomon was soon drunk. While he wasn't looking, either Brown or Hamilton placed a drug in his drink to make him even drowsier. More than a century later doctors at Tulane University Medical School in New Orleans concluded that Solomon was drugged with belladonna or laudanum, or with a mixture of both potent drugs.

When Solomon returned to Gadsby's Hotel, his head began to hurt, and he felt sick to his stomach. He lay down, but his head ached too much for him to sleep. Solomon slipped into a delirium. In the dead of night several people entered his room—he thought Hamilton and Brown were among them—

who said they were taking him to a doctor. Staggering through the streets, Solomon was led into a building, where he lost consciousness. Instead of coming to in a doctor's office, however, he awoke in the slave trader James Birch's slave pen.

Locked in his cell most of each day, Solomon had plenty of time to think. Looking back, he realized that from the morning he had met Brown and Hamilton in Saratoga Springs, the men had tried to win his confidence. They had lured him farther and farther south by convincing him that the circus offered plenty of easy money. By insisting that he obtain his free papers, they had created the illusion that they cared about his welfare. The truth was, there was no fortune to be made working for the circus. In fact, there was no circus. The whole thing had been a scheme to sell him as a slave to Birch.

What about Birch? Had he known he was buying a free man? Solomon was certain of it. But buying a free man was illegal. If it became known that Solomon was no slave, Birch would have to let him go, losing his entire investment. Birch might even be sent to prison for enslaving a black man he knew to be free. Birch had beaten Solomon savagely for claiming to be free so that he would keep quiet about it in the future.

Solomon had learned something from that beating: If he wanted to survive, he couldn't talk about being free anymore. His wisest course was to keep his eyes open for a chance to escape and to try to send word home that he had been kidnapped.

Two weeks after Solomon arrived in the slave pen, Birch and his assistant entered his cell late one night, carrying lanterns. They woke him up and ordered him to prepare to depart. Before being led outside, Solomon and four of Birch's other slaves—Clemens Ray, a young woman named Eliza, and Eliza's young daughter Emily and son Randall—were handcuffed together. As they were marched through Washington, Solomon thought about calling out for help. But the streets were practically deserted, and in a city where buying and selling slaves was legal, who would pay attention to a black man's claim that he had been kidnapped? He thought of trying to run away, but how far could he get with his left hand cuffed to Clem Ray's right hand?

Birch led the five slaves to the Potomac River, where he ordered them into the hold of a steamboat, among boxes and barrels of freight. The vessel was soon steaming down the Potomac. When it passed George Washington's tomb at Mount Vernon, the steamer tolled its bell in honor of the Father of His Country. Now that he was a slave Solomon saw things differently. It seemed odd to him that the same people who practically worshiped George Washington for winning his country's freedom thought nothing of denying slaves theirs.

In the morning Birch allowed his slaves onto the steamer's deck to eat breakfast. Some birds flying along the shore caught Solomon's eye. "I envied them," he later recalled. "I wished for wings like them."

After a two-day journey via steamboat, stagecoach, and train, Birch and his slaves arrived in Richmond, the capital of Virginia. There Birch brought Solomon, Clem, Eliza, and her two children to a slave pen operated by a Mr. Goodin.

Goodin examined the five captives. When it was Solomon's turn, Goodin felt his muscles. He also inspected his teeth and skin, as if considering the purchase of a racehorse. "Well, boy, where did you come from?" Goodin asked, after finishing his examination of Solomon.

Without stopping to recall Birch's insistence that he was a runaway slave from Georgia, Solomon answered, "From New York."

"New York!" said Goodin, aware that it was a state where

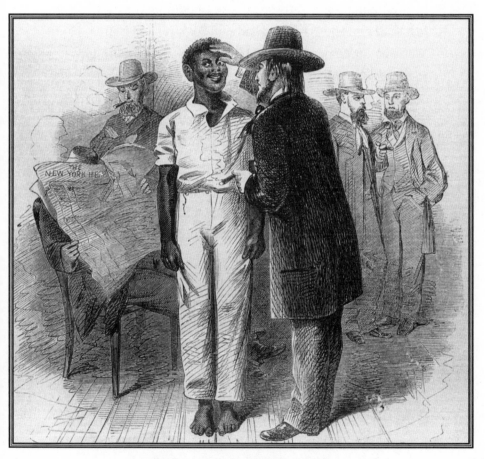

When up for sale, slaves had to act
agreeable while having their muscles and teeth inspected.
Failure to do so could result in a whipping.

many free blacks lived. "Hell, what have you been doing up there?"

Birch looked like he was about to kill him, so Solomon quickly explained that he had just been visiting New York. This seemed to satisfy Birch. For some unknown reason, Birch decided to keep Clemens Ray, whom he later took back to Washington with him.

Solomon spent only one day in Goodin's slave pen. Just as Brown and Hamilton had sold Solomon to Birch in Washington, Goodin planned to send him farther south for sale at an even higher price. The next afternoon Solomon and 40 other slaves, including Eliza and her two children, were marched onto the *Orleans*, a sailing vessel bound for New Orleans, Louisiana.

The *Orleans* floated down the James River, entered the Chesapeake Bay, then worked its way into the open waters of the Atlantic Ocean. Having studied geography, Solomon had a much better idea of their course than the other slaves did. They were heading down the East Coast, intending to reach New Orleans by sailing west around Florida.

The *Orleans* was manned only by its captain and a crew of six. They needed help with the shipboard tasks, so the slaves' handcuffs were removed and each of them was assigned a job, such as cleaning the vessel or waiting on the crew. Solomon headed the cooking unit and organized the distribution of food and water.

Off the coast of Florida the *Orleans* was battered by a violent storm that placed the ship in danger of sinking. Hoping to keep the vessel afloat, the captain sought shelter in the islands of the Bahamas. There, while they awaited a

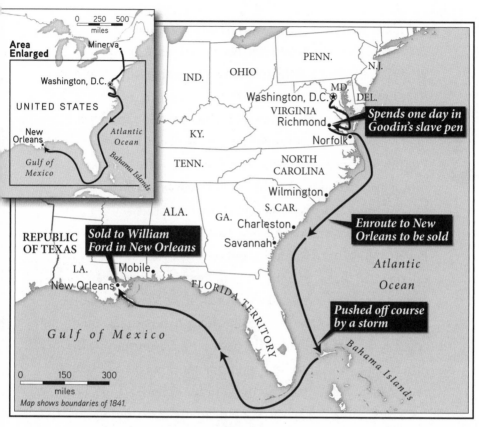

From Washington, D.C., Solomon was shipped to New Orleans,
where he was purchased by William Ford.

favorable wind to continue their journey, Solomon decided
that the time had come to make a bold strike for freedom.
He was by nature a gentle man, and the prospect of killing
members of the ship's crew repulsed him, but he knew that
he might have to do so if he ever expected to be free.

Solomon had befriended two fellow slaves on the *Orleans*
with whom he had a lot in common. One of them was another

free black man named Robert who had a wife and two children in Cincinnati, Ohio. Robert had been promised a job in Virginia, but upon arriving there he was kidnapped and sold to Goodin's slave pen in Richmond.

Arthur, his other shipboard friend, was also a free black man with a family. Arthur had been a bricklayer in Norfolk, Virginia. Late one night while returning home from work through an unfamiliar neighborhood, he was attacked by a gang of white thugs who had sold him into slavery.

Solomon discussed his plan to take over the *Orleans* with Robert and Arthur. He pointed out that when the sailors locked the slaves in the cargo hold at night, they never did a head count to make sure everyone was present. There was a small boat on the deck of the *Orleans*. By hiding beneath it, Solomon could avoid being locked in the hold at night. Then, while the others slept, he would climb out from under the little boat and release Robert and Arthur from the hold.

Next, the three of them would grab the pistols and cutlass in the captain's cabin and take the captain and crew prisoner, shooting anyone who resisted. They would then sail the ship up to New York City, where authorities were likely to sympathize with them. Solomon and his two accomplices kept their plan secret because slaves caught plotting a revolt could be put to death.

Soon after Robert and Arthur agreed to his plan, Solomon tested whether the little boat was a good hiding place. When the slaves were ordered into the hold for the night, he slipped away and hid beneath the boat. At dawn he sneaked out without anyone noticing and joined the other slaves emerging from the hold.

The three men decided to strike as soon as the *Orleans* departed the Bahamas. Finally, a favorable wind stirred, and the *Orleans* pulled up anchor and set sail. But before they could seize the vessel, Robert became ill with small-pox and died. He was buried at sea, a thousand miles from his home and family in Cincinnati. The plan for seizing control of the ship died with Robert because Solomon and Arthur could not do it by themselves.

An evening or two after Robert's death, Solomon was rest-ing on the deck when a sailor asked why he was so downhearted. The sailor, Englishman John Manning, seemed sympathetic, so Solomon decided to take a chance. He explained that he was a free man from New York with a wife and three children and that he had been kidnapped. Manning listened closely and then offered his help.

Before they parted, Solomon asked Manning to meet him in a front section of the ship called the forecastle at a certain time the following night, and to bring pen, ink, and paper with him. The next night Solomon once again avoided being locked in the hold by hiding under the little boat. In the middle of the night he crawled out and went to meet Manning.

When Solomon reached the forecastle, Manning motioned him to sit at a table where he had placed pen, ink, and paper. Solomon then began to do what very few slaves could do: write a letter. White Southerners feared that educated slaves might pass notes to each other and plan a big rebellion. That was why southern states had numerous laws forbidding slaves, and sometimes even free blacks, from learning how to read and write. White people who dared teach African Americans in defiance of the laws faced punishment themselves.

For example, in 1829 Georgia passed a law providing a fine of $500—about $12,000 in 2011 dollars—and possible imprisonment for any white man or woman who taught a black person—slave or free—to write. In 1830 Louisiana and North Carolina passed laws forbidding the teaching of reading and writing to slaves. The penalty for educating a slave in Louisiana was a year in prison. Two years later Alabama and Virginia enacted laws subjecting white people to a fine and a whipping if they were caught teaching blacks to read and write.

As a free black person growing up in New York, Solomon had obtained a fine education, so he could read and write very well. Sitting at the table with John Manning, he wrote a long letter to Henry B. Northup, a lawyer from Sandy Hill, New York, who was a member of the family that had owned Solomon's forebears. In his letter Solomon said that he had been kidnapped and was headed for New Orleans aboard the *Orleans*. Unfortunately, he didn't know who would buy him and where he would live, but he hoped Mr. Northup would inform his family that he was still alive and in the New Orleans area so they could track him down and rescue him.

John Manning promised to mail Solomon's letter from the New Orleans post office. A day or two later the ship arrived at the Crescent City with its cargo of slaves. Shortly after the *Orleans* docked, Solomon witnessed a remarkable scene. Two men boarded the vessel and informed Arthur that he was a free man and that his kidnappers had been arrested and jailed.

As he left the ship, Arthur danced about with happiness. But when Solomon looked at the crowd on the wharf, he saw no familiar faces come to liberate him.

Yet he knew he had one friend among the crew. As he left the *Orleans*, John Manning looked at Solomon over his shoulder. Solomon thought Manning's glance was to let him know that he hadn't forgotten about mailing his letter.

CHAPTER 3

"I WILL LEARN YOU YOUR NAME!"

SHORTLY AFTER THE *ORLEANS* DOCKED IN NEW ORLEANS, slave dealer Theophilus Freeman arrived on board. Freeman, who did extensive business with James Birch, had bought Solomon and several other slaves aboard the ship sight unseen. Before taking this human cargo to his slave pen, he called their names and handcuffed them.

When he called out "Platt!" no one stepped forward. Pointing to Solomon, Freeman asked the captain of the *Orleans*, "Who shipped that nigger?"

"Birch," replied the captain.

"Your name is Platt—you answer my description," said Freeman, studying his list. "Why didn't you come forward?" Solomon honestly answered that he had never been called Platt before. "Well, I will learn you your name!" said Freeman, threatening to whip Solomon if he ever again forgot that his name was Platt.

Along with the other slaves Freeman had purchased, Solomon was led to his new owner's slave pen. A portion of the pen was a kind of showroom where people shopping for slaves came to look over the merchandise. Freeman's number one rule was that his slaves must do their best to look "spry and smart" in order to attract buyers and fetch a good price. He even demanded that they dance for customers to show that they were happy to be slaves.

Solomon had been in Freeman's slave pen a day or two when an elderly gentleman came in. He lived in New Orleans, the gentleman said, and he needed a coachman. Solomon very much wanted the man to buy him, because he figured that New Orleans would offer opportunities for escape. But when Freeman announced that Solomon was selling for $1,500—equal to $40,000 today—the gentleman said that was too much and backed off.

That night Solomon came down with smallpox—the disease that had claimed Robert's life at sea. He was sent to Charity Hospital on the outskirts of New Orleans, where his condition worsened. He ran a high temperature, suffered from severe body aches, and for three days was completely blind. The doctors believed that Solomon would die, but the thought that he had to live and return to his family went round and round his feverish brain. After 16 days in the hospital he began to recover and was returned to Freeman's slave pen.

Finally, after weeks of being offered for sale, Solomon was purchased by William Ford, a planter from central Louisiana. Solomon was in such poor condition from his bout with smallpox that his selling price dropped to $900—$600 less than what he would have sold for before he became so seriously ill. He had now been sold three times: by Brown and Hamilton to Birch, by Birch to Freeman, and then by Freeman to Ford.

Slaves generally had no last names of their own but were called by their owners' last names. Platt Ford, as Solomon Northup was now known, was taken by boat, train, and on foot to William Ford's plantation. The Ford property was located in the Great Pine Woods. Escape from this vast wooded wilderness in Louisiana's Red River Valley was nearly impossible. For one thing, the area's large swamps were home to alligators and poisonous snakes. For another, the nearest "free state"—or state that had outlawed slavery—was 500 miles away.

*This is the bill of sale certifying that Theophilus Freeman
sold Solomon Northup (called Platt) to William Ford.*

Solomon was put to work chopping tree trunks into logs and making piles of lumber. A skilled carpenter, he also did construction work on the Ford family's property.

At the time, William Ford was a wealthy cotton planter who owned a number of slaves. One of them was Walton, a house slave who had lived all his life on the Ford plantation and who spoke of Mr. Ford as a child would of his father. Another was John, the Fords' 16-year-old cook, who walked around chuckling to himself and laughing at things that no one else found funny. However, Solomon felt the most sympathy for Eliza, the young woman who had been in Birch's slave pen with her two children. When Freeman sold Eliza to William Ford, he sold her son and daughter to other masters. Knowing that she probably would never see her children again, Eliza cried almost continuously.

Solomon expected that the fact that William Ford owned slaves would be reason enough to despise him. To his surprise he found that, although Ford was blind to the evils of slavery because he had been surrounded by it all his life, he also had some redeeming qualities. Every Sunday Ford gathered his slaves and read a portion of the Bible to them. Ford even broke the law by giving his slaves Bibles, and he was one of the rare masters who believed it was better to treat slaves kindly than to rule them through fear.

Solomon was even tempted to tell Mr. Ford that he had been kidnapped into slavery in the hope that he would free him. Still, Ford was a slave owner. Solomon didn't have quite enough faith in him to confide in him. Later, when he saw how cruel other masters were, Solomon realized that by not telling

*Although no photograph of Solomon Northup
is known to exist, his portrait appears in the book he wrote,*
TWELVE YEARS A SLAVE.

Ford his story he had missed a golden opportunity.

But Ford didn't remain Solomon's master for long. Several months after making slave purchases in New Orleans, he suffered financial setbacks. Among other debts, he owed John Tibaut, a traveling carpenter who was doing construction work on the Ford family's plantation, about $600. Ford and Tibaut made an unusual deal. They agreed that Solomon was worth $1,000. Ford settled his debt to the carpenter by signing over ownership of 60 percent of Solomon—a commodity worth $600—to Tibaut. However, Ford retained ownership of 40 percent of Solomon—a commodity worth $400. The fact that Ford still owned nearly half of him would mean the difference between life and death for Solomon Northup.

Now known as Platt Tibaut, Solomon had to take orders from the man who owned more than half of him. The carpenter ordered Solomon to help him complete his work on the Ford plantation. Unfortunately, Tibaut was a coldhearted taskmaster who made Solomon work from the first light of dawn until late into the night. He also continually found fault with Solomon's work and frequently cursed him out, never offering a word of encouragement. An ignorant, uneducated man, Tibaut was probably jealous of Solomon's large vocabulary and confident manner—as if he didn't think of himself as a slave.

The first serious trouble occurred when Ford was away at his summer home. Tibaut and Solomon were building a structure called a weaving house on the Ford plantation. Ford's overseer, a man named Anderson Chafin, had been left in charge of all of Ford's property, including his 40 percent ownership of Solomon. A native of the free state of Pennsylvania, Chafin disliked the way Tibaut treated Solomon.

One night Tibaut ordered him to awaken very early in the morning, ask Overseer Chafin for a keg of nails, and then use them to hammer in siding on the weaving house. Solomon did precisely as ordered. Before daylight he spoke to Chafin, who brought him a keg of nails from the plantation storeroom. "If Tibaut prefers a different size, I will furnish them," Chafin said. He then mounted his horse and went out to supervise the field slaves, while Solomon broke open the keg and began installing the siding.

A couple of hours later, Tibaut awoke and emerged from William Ford's house to inspect Solomon's work. He was in an especially foul mood and let loose a barrage of curses between complaints that the nails were the wrong size. "Goddamn you!" he yelled at Solomon. "I thought you knowed something!"

"I tried to do as you told me, master," said Solomon, doing his best to calm Tibaut. But the carpenter had worked himself into a fury. He dashed to the plantation house, grabbed a whip, then ran back and ordered Solomon to take off his shirt.

Besides feeling that he had done nothing blameworthy, Solomon had had his fill of being mistreated. "I will not!" he said, defying his master. The next moment Tibaut grabbed him by the throat and raised the whip. Solomon's pent-up rage now exploded. Before Tibaut could strike, Solomon threw him to the ground, wrestled the whip away, and began lashing him with it. Tibaut's pleas for mercy only increased Solomon's anger. Finally, Overseer Chafin heard the commotion and rode up on horseback to investigate.

The penalty for a slave striking his master was death, but Chafin blamed Tibaut for the fight. Aside from possessing a sense of justice, Chafin had to protect William Ford's 40 percent interest in Solomon.

"What is the matter with the nails?" Chafin demanded of Tibaut, after learning what had happened. When Tibaut explained that they were the wrong size, Chafin said, "I told Platt to take them and use them, and if they were not the proper size I would get others. It is not his fault."

"This is not half over yet!" said Tibaut, shaking his fist and vowing that he would have his revenge on Platt. Tibaut then saddled his horse and departed on the road to nearby Cheneyville.

Tibaut was a rascal and was up to no good, Chafin confided to Solomon. He ordered Solomon to remain on the plantation no matter what happened. Chafin then went back to supervise the field slaves.

Solomon was not proud of the fact that he had whipped his master, for he knew that he had let his temper place his life in jeopardy. He stood for some time pondering what had happened, and then he saw what he had dreaded. Coming up the road was Tibaut, accompanied by two other horsemen. The three men rode onto the Ford property, jumped off their horses, then approached Solomon holding large whips. One of the men also carried a length of rope.

The three men overpowered Solomon. They tied the rope around his wrists, ankles, and back until he couldn't move at all. With the loose end of the rope, Tibaut fashioned a noose and looped it around Solomon's neck.

"Now, then," one of Tibaut's friends said, "where shall we hang the nigger?"

Solomon frantically looked around for Chafin, who was nervously pacing back and forth on the porch of the Ford house. Was this how his life would end—hanging from a tree fifteen hundred miles from home? Tears flowed down his cheeks, but they only drew laughter from the three men who intended to murder him.

Tibaut and his friends were dragging Solomon to a tree when Anderson Chafin suddenly approached with a pistol in each hand. "Whoever moves that slave another foot is a dead man," Chafin warned. "First, he does not deserve this treatment. You, Tibaut, are a scoundrel, and you richly deserved the flogging you received. In the next place, in the absence of William Ford, I am master here. My duty is to protect his interests, and that duty I shall perform. As for you," he told Tibaut's two companions, who were overseers from nearby plantations, "begone! If you have any regard for your safety, I say, begone!"

Without saying a word, Tibaut's two friends mounted their horses and galloped away. Tibaut cursed and made a few threats before climbing on his horse and departing. Then Chafin wrote out a pass for a slave named Lawson to go by mule and notify Mr. Ford that he was needed at his plantation.

Solomon knew he had come very close to dying on that hot summer morning. He also was familiar enough with John Tibaut to know that the dispute between the two of them was far from over.

CHAPTER 4

LIFE IS DEAR TO EVERY ◄ LIVING ► THING

ANDERSON CHAFIN LEFT SOLOMON STANDING NEAR the tree where Tibaut and his friends had been about to hang him, with the noose still around his neck and his body bound by rope. When William Ford arrived, Chafin wanted him to see what Tibaut had tried to do.

A few hours later Ford galloped up the road. He spoke briefly with Chafin, then hurried over to Solomon. Taking his knife from his pocket, Ford cut the rope off Solomon, who was so exhausted from his ordeal that he could barely stand. "Thank God, Master Ford, that you have come" was all Solomon could say.

"Poor Platt, you are in a bad state," said Ford. He was heading toward his house to talk further with Chafin about the incident when Tibaut and his friends appeared on horseback. Tibaut and Ford began arguing. Although Solomon couldn't make out their exact words, he knew that Tibaut was saying that he deserved to die for fighting him, while Ford strongly disagreed. After a prolonged dispute, Tibaut and his two friends rode away.

Solomon worked by himself on the weaving house until nightfall. Then, as exhausted as he had ever been in his life, he dragged himself into his cabin. Having heard that Solomon had whipped Tibaut and lived to tell about it, the slaves with whom he shared a cabin wanted to know the details. Solomon was relating the day's events when Chafin entered the cabin.

"Tibaut intends to kill you," Chafin warned Solomon. For safety's sake, Solomon was told to spend the night in the Fords' plantation house rather than in the slave quarters.

Solomon did as he was told but found it impossible to sleep knowing that Tibaut might be lurking nearby with a gun or a knife. In the middle of the night a dog began to bark. Chafin came into Solomon's room and said, "I believe, Platt, that scoundrel is skulking about somewhere." But Tibaut did not try to take revenge on Solomon that night.

Soon nearly everyone in central Louisiana had heard about Solomon beating up Tibaut. His two owners, Ford and Tibaut, agreed that Solomon should get away from both of them for a while, so they rented him out for a month to work on the plantation of Ford's brother-in-law, Peter Tanner. At the end of the month Solomon was sent back to Tibaut, who told everyone that he had forgiven Solomon for beating him.

Not for one moment did Solomon believe that Tibaut had put their fight behind him. The first two days that the two of them worked together back on the Ford plantation, Chafin remained nearby to make sure Solomon was safe. On the third morning, convinced that the quarrel was at last over, Chafin left Tibaut and Solomon alone together to build an apparatus called a cotton press.

This was the chance Tibaut had awaited. Immediately after Chafin left, he began criticizing Solomon's work. When Solomon protested, Tibaut called him a "damned liar." Suddenly Tibaut grabbed a hatchet from the workbench. Solomon was ready. He seized Tibaut's arm, twisted the hatchet from his grasp, and hurled it into the woods.

Maddened with rage, Tibaut seized a five-foot-long wooden pole and charged Solomon with it. Before Tibaut

*A cotton press, such as the one Solomon and Tibaut built,
is a mule-powered device that was used to compress cotton
into bales for sale and shipping.*

could impale him, Solomon tackled him around the waist and
wrestled him to the ground. He pulled the pole from Tibaut
and threw it as far away as he could.

But Tibaut wasn't done. He ran for another weapon on
the workbench—a large ax with its blade buried in a wooden
plank. As Tibaut struggled to remove the blade from the piece
of wood, Solomon realized that despite the fact that he was
enslaved, life was dear to him, as it was to every living thing.

Solomon rushed Tibaut from behind, seized him by the throat, and began to choke the life out of him. As Tibaut's face turned purple, Solomon realized that if he killed his owner he would undoubtedly be put to death. Letting loose of Tibaut's neck, Solomon began to run. He leaped a nearby fence, ran past the slaves working in the cotton field, crossed a pasture, and then headed toward the Great Crocodile Swamp, a vast wetland inhabited by alligators, which at that time were often referred to as crocodiles.

Few slaves who tried to escape through the Great Crocodile Swamp made it out alive. Besides alligators, the swamp was crawling with poisonous snakes called water moccasins, and it was also inhabited by bears and wildcats. Furthermore, in places the swamp waters were deep. Since slaves weren't taught to swim, many runaways drowned.

To make things worse, Solomon heard dogs barking and horses' hooves hitting the ground. Climbing a tall fence, he saw Tibaut and two other horsemen searching for him, along with a pack of eight or ten tracking dogs. At one point the dogs came within a hundred feet of catching up to him. Solomon, however, had learned to swim growing up in New York State, so he threw the dogs off his scent by swimming underwater.

Somewhere in his flight, Solomon lost a shoe. Several times, as he waded through the swamp, he came close to stepping on an alligator or water moccasin with his bare foot. Finally, Tibaut and his friends gave up the chase. Still, Solomon kept going hour after hour, finding his way by moonlight after the sun set.

Sometime during the night he walked out of the swamp

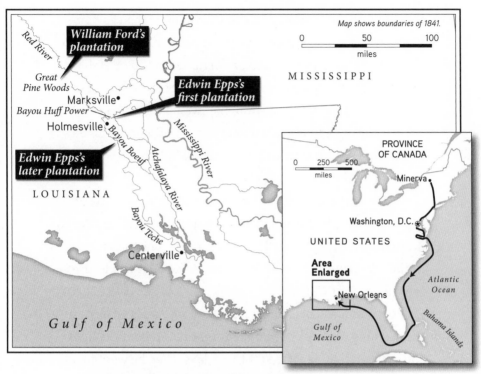

Twelve years of Solomon's life were spent in slavery along the Louisiana bayous.

into the Great Pine Woods. For a time he wandered about, searching for the Ford family's summer home, where he believed William Ford could be found. Near dawn, at a clearing in the woods, he approached a farm and saw a young white man and his slave chasing wild hogs.

Solomon was afraid that the white man might ask to see his pass, then arrest him as a runaway slave when he couldn't produce it. He was too exhausted to run any more, though, so he thought up a clever strategy. Having spent more than 24 hours in the water, Solomon looked like some kind of swamp creature. His clothing was in shreds and one of his feet was bare and punctured by thorns. Bloody scratches and bruises covered his entire body, and green slime from the swamp coated his skin.

Adopting a fierce facial expression, Solomon walked toward the young man and demanded, "Where does William Ford live?"

Eager for this frightful-looking creature to continue on his way, the startled young man answered the question. "Seven miles from here," he said. "Do you see those pine trees yonder? At their feet runs the Texas Road. Turn left, and it will lead you to William Ford's."

Solomon reached Ford's summer home at about eight in the morning. Ford asked him many questions about the fight and saw to it that he rested for three days. Then he went to talk to Tibaut, taking Solomon with him. Solomon's two owners met on the road and began discussing what had happened. Ford called it "shameful" that Tibaut had tried to kill Solomon once again, but Tibaut dismissed the incident as if it had been nothing more than a fox hunt.

"I never saw such running," said Tibaut. "Somehow the dogs got off the track, and we had to give up the hunt. We rode the horses as far as we could, and then kept on foot till the water was three feet deep. The boys said he was drowned, sure. He's a cuss to run, that nigger is!"

William Ford again insisted that Tibaut and Solomon be separated. For a few weeks Solomon's two owners rented him out to work on a plantation belonging to Ford's neighbor. Then on April 9, 1843, Solomon learned that he had been sold to a Louisiana cotton planter named Edwin Epps. His selling price had been $1,500—equal in today's money to $40,000. William Ford and John Tibaut settled up their 60/40 split and turned Solomon over to his new owner.

Platt Tibaut, formerly Platt Ford, was now Platt Epps. Except to one person to whom he revealed his real name, he would remain Platt Epps for the next decade.

CHAPTER 5

"A SONG OF PEACE"

BACK IN SARATOGA SPRINGS, NEW YORK, ANNE NORTHUP and the three children had become extremely worried when they returned home and found no trace of their husband and father. A few weeks passed before they discovered what had happened. The letter Solomon had written to Henry B. Northup when he was aboard the *Orleans* and passed to John Manning had arrived. Henry B. Northup relayed the startling news to Anne: Solomon expected to be sold as a slave in New Orleans, but he didn't know who would buy him or where he would be taken to live.

That wasn't the only information Solomon's family received about him. Clemens Ray, who had befriended Solomon in the slave pen in Washington, D.C., had later escaped and headed toward Canada. Escaped slaves were safe in that country because slavery wasn't allowed there and it was illegal for slave hunters to track fugitives onto Canadian soil.

When he was within 150 miles of Canada, Clem did something remarkable. Despite the fact that slave hunters still may have been on his own trail, he stopped in Saratoga Springs, where Solomon had told Clem he lived. Clem found Anne and, before resuming his northward journey to Canada, told her everything he knew about Solomon's kidnapping.

Anne was thankful that her husband was alive, but she now faced a huge problem. How could she discover Solomon's precise whereabouts and rescue him?

The kidnapping of free black people from New York had become such a big problem that in the spring of 1840 the state had passed a special law about it. "An Act to Protect the Free Citizens of this State from Being Kidnapped, or Reduced to Slavery" stated that if a New York inhabitant was kidnapped and taken to another U.S. state or territory, "it shall be the duty of the Governor to take such measures to procure such person to be restored to his liberty, and returned to this State."

Chief among these measures was the appointment of an "agent to collect the proper proof" that the person in question was a free black. The agent was to travel, at the state of New York's expense, to the place where the kidnap victim was being held and present evidence to help free him or her.

Thanks to this act, Anne wouldn't have to fight her battle alone. The New York state government and the governor himself were bound by law to help liberate Solomon Northup. There was an obstacle, though, and it was a big one.

Before he could be set free, Solomon had to be found. New Orleans was the nation's largest market for buying and selling slaves. As of 1841 many of Louisiana's 140,000, Mississippi's 200,000, and Alabama's 250,000 slaves had been purchased in New Orleans. Finding one person whose name was known out of those nearly 600,000 slaves would be a difficult enough task. But because Solomon had undergone so many name changes, it would be especially difficult to find him. The fact was, no one from New York knew to search for him under the name Platt. Before tracking him down, Solomon's loved ones could only wait and hope for more clues about his whereabouts.

Meanwhile, Platt Epps, as Solomon was now called, went to live at the Edwin Epps plantation on a stream called Bayou Huff Power, two and a half miles from Holmesville, Louisiana. Epps's cotton plantation was small, with only about ten slaves. Along with three or four other slaves, Solomon lived in a log cabin that had no windows and a dirt floor. When it rained, water gushed into the cabin through crevices in the ceiling and soaked everyone inside. His bed was a wooden plank, his pillow a stick of wood, and his only bedding a raggedy old blanket.

Every Sunday their week's food supply was doled out to Solomon and the other Epps slaves. It consisted of large amounts of corn and bacon. With summertime temperatures frequently topping 90°F and no refrigeration, the bacon often spoiled before the week ended, leaving the slaves with just corn to eat.

Edwin Epps was an especially harsh master. An hour before daybreak he blew a horn, signaling that it was time for the slaves to awaken and start working in the field. At midday they were allowed just ten or fifteen minutes to eat their dinner of cold bacon and corn. On bright moonlit nights Solomon and the other slaves sometimes had to work past midnight.

After their day's work finally ended, only a few hours remained for the slaves to eat their supper and get a little sleep. Often, though, Solomon was so tired when he returned from the field that he fell asleep on his wooden plank without eating a bite. Before he knew it, the horn would signal the beginning of a new workday.

Each part of the year had its special activities on the Epps plantation. Around New Year's Day the hogs were slaughtered, smoked, and made into bacon. February was the time to plant corn, which was primarily used to feed hogs and slaves. March and April were the cotton-planting months. April to July were devoted to hoeing the weeds in the cotton fields and tending the growing cotton plants. August to January were the months for picking cotton.

Master Epps managed his slaves without an overseer, relying on his whip to make them obey his rules. The slaves were whipped if they failed to show up by sunrise. They were whipped if they stopped work to talk or rest without permission. Since cotton won't grow on a broken branch, any slave who carelessly damaged a cotton plant was whipped. Another whipping offense was the failure to pick enough cotton.

In the fall, slaves in Louisiana picked cotton from sunup to sundown in the blazing sun as high temperatures baked the fields. Today, giant machines harvest the cotton.

Epps had a way to determine how much each slave was required to pick. On the first day that a new "hand" was out in the field, he or she was ordered to pick as much cotton as possible—and was encouraged to do so with a few cracks of Epps's whip. That night the new field hand's cotton was weighed. Two hundred pounds of cotton was considered a typical day's work. More was good, while less was a poor showing. A young woman belonging to Epps named Patsey often picked 500 pounds of cotton in a single day—more than twice the usual amount. Solomon, whose hands were awkward in the fields, picked only 95 pounds of cotton on his first day.

Thereafter, Solomon was expected to pick at least 95 pounds of cotton a day, just as Epps's other slaves had set standards for themselves. Each night when they took their baskets of cotton to be "toted," or weighed, the field hands trembled with fear. Those who had picked significantly less cotton than expected were whipped—the number of stripes depending on how deficient they had been in their day's work. But Epps was also hard on slaves who picked 10 or 20 pounds more cotton than usual. In that case the daily total demanded of them might be raised.

Besides punishing his slaves for breaking his rules, Epps whipped them for his personal amusement. Once a week he and other planters held shooting matches in nearby Holmesville. The men pooled their money and bought several beef cattle, which they shot at from a distance. The first marksman to kill one of the animals was the winner. He was expected to share the meat with the others so that no matter who won, everyone went home with a slab of beef.

The shooting matches ended with the men guzzling large

amounts of liquor. As a result, they returned home drunk. On such occasions Epps would stumble around his house breaking dishes and glasses against the walls. His wife, Mary, would threaten to leave him and return to her father's house in Cheneyville, but after a while she couldn't help laughing at her husband's drunken pranks.

Once he had his fill of throwing things around his house, Epps would go outside with his whip and yell for his slaves to come out to the yard. He would make them run around while he chased after them, trying to lash any who wandered too close to his whip.

But most often Epps returned from Holmesville in a dancing mood. Somewhere Mary Epps had heard that Solomon played the violin. At her request Master Epps bought Solomon a fiddle on a trip to New Orleans. Epps would order Solomon to get his violin and play a lively tune while the slaves danced in the yard.

"Dance, you damned niggers, dance!" the drunken master would order, cracking his whip around their ears to keep them moving. With his whip in his hand, he would dance along with them. If a slave stopped for a moment to rest or catch his breath—CRACK!—down came the whip. If Solomon began to nod off while fiddling, he would be awakened by the sting of leather on his skin. Sometimes Epps forced his slaves to dance most of the night, leaving only an hour or two before they had to be back in the cotton field.

Edwin and Mary Epps had a ten-year-old son who enjoyed "playing overseer." Carrying a miniature whip, he would ride his pony into the cotton field. The boy would inflict lashes on the slaves, all the while cursing at them and shouting for them to work faster. Master Epps would laugh at his son's antics and praise him for following in his footsteps. What struck Solomon about young Epps was that he seemed to be an otherwise intelligent boy. But slavery was a fact of his life and he was learning to be a slave owner from his father, so it never occurred to him that what he was doing might be wrong.

The plantation on Bayou Huff Power did not actually belong to Edwin Epps. The owner, an uncle of Mary Epps, rented it to Edwin. In late 1844 a rumor reached the slave quarters. Having made a handsome profit from his cotton crops, Edwin Epps had bought a plantation of his own and was moving his family and slaves there.

When he first heard about it, Solomon Northup was elated. Every day over the past two years he had thought about escaping, but he hadn't seen an opportunity. Moving to a new location had to be a change for the better—or so Solomon hoped.

Edwin Epps moved his family and slaves to the new plantation in early 1845. Solomon was deeply disappointed to find that the new place was in a swampy area along a stream called Bayou Boeuf. It was as remote and as difficult a locale to escape from as any place in Louisiana. Solomon had now been a slave for four years, and although he wasn't about to give up, he couldn't help wondering if he'd ever find a way to return to his family.

The companionship of his fellow slaves helped Solomon endure his life in bondage. As a free black man, he had always looked down on slaves as inferior to himself. Now he saw how wrong he had been. Although deprived of education, slaves had a native intelligence and good sense that helped them survive.

Central Louisiana, where Solomon was enslaved, is webbed with many bayous—swamps and marshes fed by slow-moving flatland streams.

The way they looked out for one another was touching. And while they were no substitute for his wife and children, they were the closest thing he had to a family.

Solomon had several friends among Epps's slaves. The elder among them was a very tall man known as Old Abram. There wwas a saying in Louisiana that gray-haired black people were rare around Bayou Boeuf because most slaves died young of illness and overwork. Abram, who was in his 60s, was an exception to the rule.

Once known for his enormous strength, Abram had formerly belonged to a soldier who served under famed Indian fighter Andrew Jackson, later the seventh President of the United States. Abram was never happier than when his fellow slaves sat around him as he related stories about Old Hickory Jackson's brave fighting. In fact, Abram was better at recalling details of 30-year-old battles than he was at keeping track of where he had left his hat or his hoe.

Slowing down both physically and mentally, Old Abram was still expected to work a full day in the cotton fields. He became something of a father figure to Solomon, who grew attached to the old man.

Phebe and Wiley were a married couple who were both close to 50 years of age. Phebe was the Epps family's cook. Because she worked in her owner's "big house," Phebe heard many of the white people's conversations, which she reported to the other slaves. Wiley was a very quiet man. Because Wiley rarely shared his thoughts with anyone, Solomon was slow to realize that Wiley and he had something in common—a powerful desire to escape.

Phebe and Wiley had a 13-year-old son named Edward. By an earlier marriage, Phebe had two other sons who also belonged to Epps. Bob and Henry were probably in their teens when the move was made to Bayou Boeuf.

Perhaps because she reminded him of his own daughters, a young woman in her early 20s won a special place in Solomon's heart. Patsey did not think of herself as a slave. She was proud of the fact that she was close to her African origins, her mother having been brought over on a slave ship. She also took great pride in being the "queen of the field" at cotton-picking time, often picking 500 pounds in a single day. But while Patsey appeared to be a lighthearted girl who rejoiced in just being alive, Solomon discovered that she suffered more than anyone else at the hands of Edwin Epps. Over the years Solomon did his best to make her life less difficult.

Something else provided solace for Solomon: his violin. He played it on many more pleasant occasions than the times Epps returned home from the shooting contests and made him fiddle a tune while the other slaves danced.

Mrs. Epps fancied herself an appreciator of fine music. She frequently invited Platt into the big house parlor, then gathered her entire family to hear him play. Other families along Bayou Boeuf heard about the slave who played the violin so beautifully. Neighbors began asking Edwin Epps if they could rent Platt to play at their balls and parties. Though Epps got the rental fee, usually the partygoers showed their appreciation for Solomon's playing by showering him with picayunes—Spanish coins worth about six cents apiece that were popular in the South in the 1800s. Solomon was allowed to keep this money, which eventually added up to several dollars.

The favorite time of year for most slaves was Christmas week, when masters gave their slaves a few days off so that they could visit relatives and friends on nearby plantations. Planters also took turns hosting huge Christmas parties that might include more than a hundred slaves in an area. A Christmas party featured foods the slaves rarely got to eat, as well as music and dancing. During a typical Christmas week Solomon might play at three parties, traveling from plantation to plantation and filling his pockets with picayunes.

But except for crickets and frogs, no audience attended Solomon's most special moments with his violin. Often, in the middle of the night, when he couldn't sleep because he felt troubled, Solomon would creep out of the cabin to the bank of the stream. There in the tall grass he would play what he called a song of peace that reminded him of home.

CHAPTER 6

"IF I EVER CATCH YOU WITH WITH A BOOK"

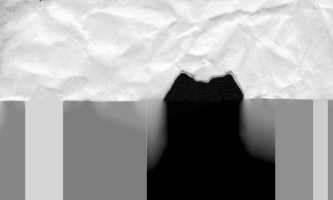

I N 1845—THE FIRST YEAR EDWIN EPPS HAD HIS OWN
plantation on Bayou Boeuf—caterpillars almost totally
destroyed the region's cotton crop. To recoup some of their
losses, many cotton planters rented out a number of their
slaves to work in the sugarcane fields of far southern Louisiana.

That fall 150 slaves from various Holmesville-area farms
walked a hundred miles to the Centerville area near the Gulf
of Mexico. There they were put to work harvesting sugarcane.
Among the slaves who made the long walk were Old Abram,
Bob, and Platt from the Epps plantation. Solomon was put in
charge of about 75 cane cutters, as the field hands who harvested
the crop were called.

Solomon brought his violin along—and his reputation for playing it. One weekend he was hired to perform at
a party in Centerville. The partygoers were so pleased with
his playing that at the close of the festivities they took up a
collection for Solomon that totaled $17—equal to more than
$400 in today's money.

Solomon had a secret plan for spending the money.
Centerville was a stopping place for steamboats traveling along
a stream called Bayou Teche. From there they steamed to New
Orleans, 75 miles away. If he could make it to the big city of
New Orleans, Solomon believed he could find a way to travel
north to the free states.

Because of his violin playing, Solomon was provided with
passes permitting him to move about Centerville to arrange
his performances. Somewhere in town he heard that a certain

Cane sugar is a tall, very sweet grass that grows in Louisiana. Like cotton, it is now machine-harvested. Sugarcane can grow as high as 19 feet.

steamboat captain who stopped there regularly was a Northerner opposed to slavery. One day Solomon went to the docks on Bayou Teche and quietly spoke to this captain.

Solomon got right to the point. Would the captain let him hide among the cargo so that he could escape to New Orleans? To grease the way, Solomon offered some of the money he had earned from fiddling.

The steamboat captain seemed willing to assist Solomon, but he explained why he couldn't take part in such a plan. In

New Orleans vessels were thoroughly searched for stowaway fugitive slaves. If Solomon were discovered hiding on the steamer and it was revealed that the captain had helped hide him, his vessel could be seized and he could be jailed. He was sorry, the captain said, but he couldn't help Solomon escape.

Another five years passed before Solomon had another genuine opportunity to inform the outside world of his whereabouts. Mrs. Mary Epps liked Solomon and had him run errands for her when her husband was away. In 1850 when Edwin Epps was in New Orleans selling his cotton crop, his wife sent Solomon to a store in Holmesville to buy several items, including a block of paper.

Before he brought Mrs. Epps's purchases into the big house for her, Solomon took a sheet or two of the paper for himself. He hid it in his cabin beneath the board he slept on. This was the first writing paper Solomon obtained in the nine years he had been a slave.

He made a pen by plucking a large feather out of a duck's wing. Solomon made ink by boiling white maple bark. Then, when everyone else in his cabin was asleep, Solomon took the paper, pen, and ink from beneath the plank and began writing by the light of the fireplace. Over a period of a few days he wrote a letter chronicling how he'd been kidnapped into slavery and explaining that he was on the Epps plantation in the vicinity of Holmesville and Marksville, Louisiana.

Now came the hard part—mailing the letter. In the South, postmasters would not mail letters given to them by slaves unless they were accompanied by notes from their owners. This meant that Solomon had to find a white person who would mail his letter for him. He found a likely candidate—he believed—months later when a poor, white man named Armsby came into the area seeking a job as an overseer. Epps and other planters turned Armsby down. He became so desperate for a job that for a small salary he went to work alongside the slaves in the fields of a neighbor of Epps named Shaw.

Armsby liked to fall asleep at night out on the porch of Shaw's home. At 1 a.m. on a warm night, Solomon left the Epps plantation without permission and walked to the Shaw place, where Armsby was sleeping. He awoke Armsby and asked if he would mail a letter for him at Marksville, 20 miles away. As an incentive, he offered Armsby all the money he had earned by playing his violin. Armsby agreed to the deal, promising to mail Solomon's letter at the Marksville post office.

Something about Armsby made Solomon uneasy. So despite the fact that the letter was in his pocket, Solomon told Armsby he would bring the letter to him along with the money in a few days.

Solomon's mistrust of Armsby was well founded, for a day or two later he saw Armsby and Epps sitting together on a fence that divided the Shaw and the Epps plantations. The two men were talking—what about Solomon was fairly certain he knew.

That evening Solomon was cooking his bacon in the fireplace when Epps suddenly burst into the cabin carrying a whip. "Well, boy," he said to Solomon, who was by then 42 years old. "I understand I've got a lar-ned nigger, that writes letters, and tries to get white fellows to mail 'em. Wonder if you know who he is?"

"Don't know nothing about it, Master Epps," answered Solomon, venturing into dangerous territory. A slave's word was almost never believed over a white person's, and if it came out that Solomon was lying—which he was—he would be in for a terrible whipping. Solomon had something else against him. Right after buying him, Epps had grown suspicious that Solomon had been educated somewhere because of the way he spoke. Epps had even warned him: "If I ever catch you with a book, or with pen and ink, I will give you a hundred lashes!"

Epps demanded to know: "Weren't you over to Shaw's night before last? Haven't you asked that fellow Armsby to mail a letter for you at Marksville? What have you got to say to that?"

Solomon denied all of Armsby's accusations and countered with a plausible explanation. "How could I write a letter without any ink or paper? That Armsby is a lying, drunken fellow. Didn't he want you to hire him for an overseer?" By making up a lie that one of Epps's slaves needed close watching, Armsby was still trying to get Epps to hire him as an overseer, Solomon concluded.

Solomon held his breath as Epps thought over what he had said. Finally, Epps answered, "I'm damned, Platt, if I don't believe you tell the truth." Still clutching his whip, Epps left the cabin. Solomon waited until the other slaves in the cabin were asleep, then he pulled out his letter and with a heavy heart threw it into the fireplace.

A few days earlier Solomon had been filled with hope. Now after nine years he was no closer to freedom than he had been on the day he awoke in the slave pen in Washington, D.C.

This early 1860s photo of slave quarters on a sugarcane plantation was taken in Houma, Louisiana, not far from where Solomon supervised 75 cane cutters.

At this time Epps was often drunk, and he was mistreating his slaves more than ever. Hardly any of his slaves escaped punishment—even those who weren't guilty of breaking his rules.

One day when Mrs. Epps sent Solomon on an errand to a neighboring plantation, he returned to find a horrifying sight. Old Abram was lying on the cabin floor in a pool of his own blood. The old man told Solomon that he had been placing wet cotton on a platform to dry out when Epps came home drunk from Holmesville. Epps began yelling at Abram for no particular reason, and the old man became so confused that he made some small mistake in handling the cotton. Flying into a rage, Epps pulled out his knife and stabbed Old Abram in the back.

Fortunately, the wound was not deep enough to be fatal. As Mrs. Epps sewed it up, she scolded her husband. If he didn't change his ways, she warned, he would eventually kill all their slaves in his drunken rages.

On several occasions when Phebe angered Epps, he picked up a chair and smashed it over her head. Phebe's husband Wiley was also the target of their master's wrath. One night Wiley visited a friend on a neighboring plantation without obtaining a pass. The patrollers who rode about looking for runaway slaves chased him down with their dogs, one of which sank its teeth into his leg. The patrollers whipped Wiley and brought him back to Epps, who gave him a ferocious beating.

Unable to tolerate any more abuse, Wiley ran away. Epps vowed that when Wiley was caught, he would make him sorry he had ever been born. For weeks Wiley evaded capture, but after nearly a month he was caught and locked in jail. Epps paid the fee to have Wiley released and whipped him so brutally that he was crushed in both body and spirit. Wiley never tried to run away again.

But it was Patsey who received the most abuse. Edwin and Mary Epps both tormented her. Epps wanted Patsey to have sex with him, but she refused, which enraged him. Mary Epps was jealous of her husband's interest in Patsey and tried to spite her whenever she had a chance. Solomon did what little he could to protect Patsey, and that brought their master's wrath down upon him, too.

One day Patsey and Solomon were hoeing the ground when Epps returned home drunk from a shooting match in Holmesville. Epps stood on the edge of the field motioning to

Patsey. "Platt," said Patsey, "do you see old Hog Jaw beckoning me to come to him?"

With a quick glance, Solomon saw Epps gesturing to Patsey, who began to cry. She should keep working and act as though she hadn't seen Epps, Solomon advised. But despite being drunk, Epps noticed that Solomon had said something to Patsey. Staggering up to Solomon, he demanded, "What did you say to Pats?"

Solomon didn't answer the question, which made Epps even angrier. Suddenly he pulled his knife out of his pocket and tried to stab Solomon, as he had Old Abram. Solomon jumped out of the way. Shouting "I'll cut your black throat!" Epps chased him around the field for the next hour. Only when Mrs. Epps came out of the house and told her husband to stop did he put his knife away.

Patsey was at the center of an even more disturbing incident involving Solomon. On Sundays the slaves took their dirty laundry down to Bayou Boeuf to wash it. One Sunday Mary Epps gave all the slaves except Patsey pieces of soap for the clothes washing.

Rather than make a big issue about a piece of soap, Patsey walked a short way to the Shaw plantation. She borrowed some soap from a friend, then began to wash her dirty laundry in the stream with the other slaves. What Patsey didn't know was that Epps had been spying on his slaves from a distance and had seen her leave without permission. For going off on her own, Epps ordered that she be whipped—and that Solomon inflict the punishment. If Solomon refused, said Epps, he would personally give both Patsey and Solomon the beating of their lives.

Realizing that he was left with no choice, Solomon took the whip from Epps as Patsey was tied to stakes in the ground. Then he began lashing Patsey—trying to inflict as little suffering upon her as he could.

"Strike harder!" Epps warned Solomon. "Strike harder, or your turn will come next, you scoundrel!" Meanwhile, Mary Epps watched from her porch with a look of satisfaction.

After lashing Patsey until her back was covered with blood, Solomon felt sick about what he had done. He threw the whip down and announced that he would beat Patsey no more, whatever the consequences. Epps grabbed the whip and lashed Patsey with it until she lost consciousness. Then he ordered Solomon to take Patsey to her cabin.

After that, Patsey was never the same. Often in her sleep she would sit up and plead for mercy, as she relived the terrible beating in her nightmares. Although she never blamed Solomon for what had happened, she lost her zest for life and began to brood most of the time. The other slaves said that Patsey was suffering from a broken heart.

Another heart was broken because of Patsey's whipping: Solomon Northup's.

CHAPTER 7

"I AM HERE NOW A SLAVE"

BY THE SUMMER OF 1852, ELEVEN YEARS HAD PASSED since Solomon Northup had been stolen into slavery. While his family in New York still nursed hope that he would one day return to them, they knew that the chances of this happening were slim. Solomon and Anne's three children—Elizabeth, Margaret, and Alonzo—had only dim memories of the father who had disappeared when they were very young. Now 20, 18, and 16 years old respectively, they had begun their own lives. Margaret had married and was a mother. Little Solomon Northup Staunton had been named for the grandfather who didn't even know of his existence.

Solomon Northup was now 44 years old—an age not often attained by slaves in Louisiana because of all the hardships and diseases they were subject to. As events from his years as a free man faded deeper into the past, his former life sometimes seemed like a dream. Yet in his soul there remained a flicker of hope that one day he would regain his freedom.

In June of 1852 Edwin Epps hired a crew of carpenters to build a new house for his family. Epps knew that Platt had done carpentry work under Tibaut, so he pulled him from the field and ordered him to help a carpenter named Samuel Bass construct the house.

By listening to white people's conversations, Solomon learned about Bass's background. About 45 years old, Bass was just a little older than he was. Born in Canada, he had married a woman named Lydia, with whom he had four daughters. However, 15 years earlier he and his wife had separated, and he had rarely seen his daughters since then. Bass seemed to be a sad man who roamed about doing odd jobs without much purpose in life. His travels had eventually taken him more than a thousand miles south of Canada to Marksville, Louisiana, where he lived while helping to build Edwin Epps's new house.

Among the planters along Bayou Boeuf, Samuel Bass was known for loving to argue. Whatever the subject, he had an opinion about it that usually opposed the popular view in Louisiana. Once or twice Solomon heard him talk passionately against slavery, which he claimed was "all wrong." Outsiders who expressed such unorthodox views risked being run out of Louisiana, but Samuel Bass was forgiven because it was thought that he just liked to stir up a good argument. Besides, he always listened politely to the other person's point of view.

After overhearing Bass talk about slavery with Epps and other neighbors, Solomon concluded that the carpenter wasn't arguing just to hear his own voice. He seemed to truly hate slavery. This was confirmed one day when Epps came to watch Bass and Solomon work and the two white men got into a dispute.

"It's all wrong," Bass told Epps. "I wouldn't own a slave if I was rich, which I am not. When you come down to the point, what right have you to your slaves?"

"What right?" Epps repeated with a laugh. "Why, I bought 'em, and paid for 'em."

Bass countered by saying that just because the law allowed slavery, that didn't make it right. There was a higher law—the law of right and wrong—that said slavery was evil.

"In the sight of God, what is the difference, Epps, between a white man and a black one? You have no more right to your freedom, in exact justice, than Old Abram yonder."

Epps chuckled and said, "Hope you don't compare me to a nigger, Bass."

"Look here, Epps, you can't laugh me down that way," Bass said with a touch of annoyance. "There's a fearful sin resting on this nation that will not go unpunished forever. There will be a reckoning—yes, Epps, there's a day coming that will burn as an oven. It may be sooner or it may be later, but it's a-comin' as sure as the Lord is just."

William Lloyd Garrison, a famous abolitionist leader, is pictured here being dragged through the streets by a pro-slavery mob during the Boston Riots of 1835. Garrison was the publisher of the anti-slavery newspaper The Liberator *and a founder of the American Anti-Slavery Society.*

Epps concluded his argument by saying that Bass sounded like one of those "abolitionist fanatics" from the northern states and Canada who wanted to end slavery completely. Bass didn't deny it. Then Epps got in the last word by saying that Bass loved to hear himself talk more than any man he had ever known.

While working with Samuel Bass all through the summer of 1852, Solomon became increasingly convinced that Bass truly hated slavery and might help him escape. Several times Solomon nearly told Bass how he had been kidnapped. But usually other carpenters were also working on the house, and Solomon didn't want them to overhear him talking about how he deserved his freedom. Besides, his experience with Armsby had made him extremely cautious. What if he told Bass his story, and Bass tried to get in good with Epps by repeating the story to him? Even if Bass sympathized with Solomon, would he risk his own freedom to help him?

By early August the other carpenters had completed their tasks and were gone. Epps was preoccupied with his slaves in the field and no longer had time to stop by and watch Bass and Solomon work. As he and Bass sawed and hammered at the new house with no one else around, Solomon decided to throw caution to the wind and trust that Samuel Bass was as firm about "justice" and "freedom" as he appeared to be.

One afternoon in late summer Solomon broke the rule that said a slave shouldn't speak to a white person unless spoken to. "Master Bass, I want to ask you where you came from?" Solomon asked matter-of-factly.

Samuel Bass didn't seem to mind Solomon having an informal conversation with him. He had been born in a country called Canada, Bass explained, adding that Solomon probably didn't know where that was.

"Oh, I know where Canada is," Solomon answered. He then named some of the places he had visited in Canada— Montreal, Kingston, Queenston, and elsewhere. "And I have been in New York state, too," Solomon continued. "In Buffalo and Rochester and Albany—and I can tell you the names of the villages on the Erie Canal."

Bass stared at Solomon with an expression of astonishment, for very few slaves except runaways ever visited Canada, where slavery had been outlawed nearly 20 years earlier. The same was true of New York State, where slavery had been banned for 25 years. If Solomon had really visited all the places he claimed to have seen in Canada and New York State, he probably had once been a free man.

"How came you here?" Samuel Bass finally asked Solomon in a whisper.

That was the opening Solomon Northup had awaited. "Master Bass," he said, "if justice had been done, I never would have been here."

Suddenly Samuel Bass became keenly interested in Solomon's past life. Promising not to repeat anything they discussed to Epps or anyone else, Bass asked Solomon how he had come to be a slave in Louisiana. His story would require quite a while to tell, Solomon answered. He suggested that they meet in the unfinished house around midnight, when he would relate everything to Bass.

*The Epps house that Solomon helped build has been
reconstructed and relocated to the Alexandria campus
of Louisiana State University.*

At the appointed hour Bass didn't have far to go, for that
summer he usually slept in the new house he and Solomon
were building, visiting his residence 20 miles away in
Marksville only now and then. At about midnight Solomon
crept out of his cabin in the slave quarters. Entering the
unfinished house, he found Samuel Bass waiting for him.

Deep into the night Solomon told his life story to Samuel
Bass, who listened closely and asked many questions. After

Solomon finished, Bass asked how he could help him gain his liberty. By writing and mailing letters to some of his friends in Saratoga Springs, Solomon answered. Bass said he would gladly do so. Before parting, the two men agreed to meet the next night in the tall weeds along Bayou Boeuf to begin their letter-writing campaign.

The next day Solomon obtained a piece of a candle and a few matches. Phebe, the Epps family's cook, may have smuggled these items out of the old house to him. Late that night Solomon went to the meeting place with the candle and matches. Samuel Bass arrived around the same time as Solomon. With him he brought paper and pencil that he kept in his tool chest.

Sending a letter to just one person in New York State wouldn't be sufficient, the two men figured. So many years had passed that people Solomon had known could have died or moved away. They decided to send letters to several people who might help free Solomon. Since Epps might punish Solomon severely if he caught him writing letters, they also decided that Bass should write the letters in the privacy of his Marksville residence. But first Solomon must provide names and addresses.

By the flickering candlelight Samuel Bass wrote the names and addresses of three men in Saratoga Springs as Solomon recited the information: store owners William Perry and Cephas Parker, and Judge Marvin, who had employed Solomon at the United States Hotel. All three could vouch that Solomon Northup was a free man.

Even after Bass wrote down the three men's names and

addresses, he and Solomon remained on the riverbank. Now certain that he could trust Samuel Bass, Solomon poured out his heart to him. He told Bass how much it would mean to him to see his wife and children again—even if it was just once before he died. He clasped Samuel Bass's hand and blessed him for his help. He also told Bass what for 11 years he had not told anyone. His real name wasn't Platt. It was Solomon Northup.

Bass was moved by Solomon's words and by the depth of his emotion. He confessed to Solomon that he had lived a lonely life, separated from his family and without friends. He was getting older, he said, and he didn't want to die without ever having done anything of value in the world. From this night forward he would dedicate his life to liberating Solomon and to ending the evil practice of slavery.

Before they parted, Bass warned that they must avoid talking to each other when other people were around— if Epps got wind of their plot it would be disastrous. Bass repeated that he would write and mail the letters at Marksville. Once he sent them out, he would find a way to speak privately to Solomon about it.

A few days later, on Saturday night, Samuel Bass rode to Marksville, where he lived in a rented room. He spent all day Sunday writing letters to Solomon's acquaintances in Saratoga Springs—one to Judge Marvin and another letter that was addressed jointly to William Perry and Cephas Parker. This second letter read:

Bayou Boeuf

August 15, 1852

Mr. William Perry or Mr. Cephas Parker:

GENTLEMEN—Having been born free, I am certain you must know me, and I am here now a slave. I wish you to obtain free papers for me, and forward them to me at Marksville, Louisiana. The way I came to be a slave, I was taken sick in Washington. When I recovered, I was robbed of my free-papers, and in irons on my way to this State, and have never been able to write until now; and he that is writing for me runs the risk of his life if detected.

Yours,

SOLOMON NORTHUP

Upon Bass's return from Marksville, he and Solomon resumed their work on the house, hardly speaking to one another during the course of the day. However, they soon had another midnight meeting alongside the river. The news was good, Bass told Solomon. He had written and mailed the letters without any problems. Now they could only await an answer.

Compared to today, mail delivery was slow in the 1850s. The letter might take two weeks to arrive in Saratoga Springs, New York, Bass figured, and another two weeks for a response to reach Marksville, Louisiana. In about a month—at the most six weeks—the process of freeing Solomon should be under way.

As the days passed, Solomon's excitement grew. Could it be that after 11 years as a slave he would soon be free? He liked to think of Judge Marvin, William Perry, and Cephas Parker reading the letters and spreading the word that Solomon was alive on a plantation in Louisiana. He liked to think of the moment he would once again see Anne and his children. He became so excited that he couldn't sleep or think of anything except saying goodbye to slavery.

At the end of four weeks, Samuel Bass rode to Marksville to check his mail. There was nothing for him from New York State. Seeing how disappointed Solomon was, Bass reminded him that they had figured it might take six weeks for a response to arrive.

Samuel Bass visited Marksville once more after six weeks had elapsed. Again, he had no letters from New York State. Solomon was crushed by this bad news, but Bass told him not to give up because the mail was frequently delayed for one reason or another.

Bass again rode to Marksville at the eight-week point. Again he returned with no letters in his pockets, which was also what happened after ten weeks. To make things worse, at about this time Bass and Solomon completed the Epps house. This meant that Bass had to move on to another job, and Solomon would be sent back to the cotton fields.

One last time before he departed, Samuel Bass met with Solomon by the riverside. He must not give in to despair, Bass told Solomon. Bass promised that on the day before Christmas he would pay a visit to the Epps family. At that time he would once more check his mail at the Marksville post office. If nothing had arrived from Saratoga Springs by then, he would find some other way to free Solomon.

Never had Solomon Northup looked forward to Christmas as eagerly as he did in the final weeks of 1852.

CHAPTER 8

"HOW CAN I END MY DAYS HERE?"

IME SEEMED TO SLOW TO A CRAWL FOR SOLOMON AS the day approached that Samuel Bass was supposed to return. On Friday, December 24, Solomon picked cotton with the other Epps slaves, but he kept looking up the road for a man on horseback. The noon hour came and went, with no sign of Bass. By late afternoon the sun was low in the sky, and still Bass had not appeared.

Solomon had faith in Bass's intentions, but he was worried that he couldn't keep his promise about visiting the Epps family on Christmas Eve. There were many reasons why the carpenter might not have been able to return. What if he had found a job so far from Louisiana that making the trip was too difficult? What if he had gotten sick and died? What if his role in the effort to free Solomon had been discovered? The more Solomon thought about it, the more reasons he imagined as to why Samuel Bass wouldn't appear.

Just as the sun was setting on that Christmas Eve, Solomon heard the pounding of a horse's hooves. He looked up from picking cotton, and there was the most wonderful sight he had ever beheld: Samuel Bass riding up the road to the Epps house.

Southern planters of the 19th century were famous for their hospitality. Friends, relatives, friends of relatives, and even strangers passing through could stop at almost any southern plantation and be provided with a meal and a warm bed. Edwin Epps came out to the yard to greet Bass and to invite him into the house that he and Solomon had finished building a few weeks earlier.

Of course Solomon was eager to speak to Bass alone to find out if he had received a letter from New York State. At this time Solomon shared a cabin with Old Abram and Phebe's son Bob. Around ten o'clock at night Solomon lay down on his board and pretended to fall asleep. When he was convinced that Old Abram and Bob were sleeping, Solomon went out the door. For two hours he prowled about looking for Bass in the yard and at their old meeting place in the tall grass by the riverside.

Bass did not appear, however, and by about midnight Solomon saw that the candles were still shining brightly in the Epps house. He figured that Bass was engaged in conversation with Edwin Epps and couldn't get away, but that the carpenter might attempt to speak to him early Christmas morning before his hosts awakened.

Solomon was too excited to sleep that night. Well before sunrise his two cabin mates got up to do some chores that were their responsibility even on Christmas Day. Old Abram went to start the fire in the fireplace for the Epps family. Bob fed the mules. Solomon planned to go outside to search for Bass as soon as Old Abram and Bob were gone, but he didn't have to. Bass had been hiding behind the cabin and darted inside the moment Solomon was alone.

After greeting Solomon, Bass explained that on his way to the Epps plantation he had stopped at the Marksville Post Office. "No letter yet," said Bass. Although deeply disappointed, Solomon had prepared for such an eventuality. He told Bass that he had made a mental list of other people who were likely to help free him.

"No use," said Bass. He had visited the post office in Marksville so often asking about letters from New York State that he feared the postmaster had become suspicious. "Too dangerous," Bass said about sending out more letters.

It was Chrismas Day of 1852—Solomon and Anne's twenty-third wedding anniversary—and freedom was as distant a dream as it had been in Birch's slave pen 12 years earlier. For a moment he gave in to despair. "It is all over!" Solomon said tearfully. "Oh, my God! How can I end my days here?"

He wasn't going to end his days there, Samuel Bass assured him. If Solomon could be patient for a few more months, Bass had a plan that was better than writing letters. He had a couple of carpentry jobs scheduled that would be completed by spring of 1853. "By that time I shall have a considerable sum of money, and then, Platt, I am going to Saratoga Springs myself."

Despair instantly changed into hope, thanks to Bass's generous offer. Seeing that Solomon hadn't realized to what lengths he was willing to go to free him, Bass offered an explanation. "I'm tired of slavery as much as you," he said. "If I can succeed in getting you away from here, it will be a good act that I shall like to think of all of my life."

He must hurry back to the new Epps house before he was discovered missing, Bass told Solomon. But in two months he would return. In the meantime Solomon should finish his mental list of Saratoga Springs people who might help him. Upon his return Bass would write down their names and addresses so that he could seek them out when he visited Saratoga Springs.

"Don't be discouraged!" Samuel Bass reassured Solomon. "I'm with you, life or death. God bless you!" And with that, he left the slave cabin and returned to the Epps house.

It was now the slaves' favorite time of year: Christmas Day. As in previous years, Edwin Epps granted his slaves a few days off at Christmastime to attend parties and visit friends and relatives on nearby plantations. But for Solomon Northup, Christmas provided no rest. Master Epps had received many requests to rent him out to perform at holiday parties.

For the next few days Solomon visited several plantations along Bayou Boeuf. At each place he played his violin nearly until sunrise, then slept an hour or two in the slave quarters before moving on to his next engagement. Solomon filled his pockets with coins that white people threw his way, but he became increasingly exhausted.

After a few days of playing his violin, Solomon was expected back in Epps's cotton field to resume work on Thursday morning, December 30, 1852. He was so exhausted that he barely made it out to the field by sunrise. He struggled to stay awake picking cotton on Thursday and Friday. On Saturday—New Year's Day of 1853—he overslept for the first time in years and arrived in the cotton field 15 minutes late. Epps was waiting with his whip. He ordered Solomon to remove his shirt and gave him 15 lashes—one for each minute he was late. With a back that was cut and bruised, Solomon spent Saturday picking cotton.

The next workday, Monday, January 3, 1853, Solomon made it out to the field on time. He, Old Abram, Patsey, Wiley, and Bob were picking cotton and placing it in bags tied to their necks. It was a very cold morning and their fingers grew so numb that Solomon and the others had trouble picking the cotton. Even Patsey wasn't her usual nimble-fingered self.

Epps had come out to supervise his slaves, but he had forgotten something. Saying they would all get a "good warming" within a few minutes, he hurried back inside his house to fetch his whip.

Epps hadn't yet returned when a carriage drove up to his home. Two white men stepped out of the vehicle, but they didn't go inside the house. Instead they walked toward the little group of slaves watching from the cotton field.

CHAPTER 9

"SOLOMON NORTHUP IS MY NAME!"

Solomon Northup

UNKNOWN TO SOLOMON NORTHUP AND SAMUEL BASS, their letter-writing campaign had gone better—although much slower—than they believed. Bass had expected that the letters he had written would take two weeks, perhaps a little longer, to travel 1,500 miles between Marksville, Louisiana, and Saratoga Springs, New York. Actually, both towns were off the beaten path and so the letters Bass mailed from the Marksville post office on August 15, 1852, didn't reach Saratoga Springs for nearly a month.

What became of the letter to Judge Marvin is unknown, but the letter addressed jointly to William Perry and Cephas Parker arrived safely. However, the two store owners were reluctant to become involved in such a complex and dangerous enterprise as rescuing Solomon from slavery. They forwarded the letter to Solomon's wife, Anne, who ran the kitchen at Carpenter's Hotel in Glens Falls, New York. Anne and all three of the children, including married daughter Margaret, now lived in this town near Saratoga Springs.

When Anne saw the letter from her husband, she was beside herself with excitement, as were Elizabeth, Margaret, and Alonzo. Since John Manning's letter had arrived 12 years earlier and Clem Ray had visited them a little later, Solomon's family had not heard anything whatsoever about his whereabouts. Now out of the blue came the news: Solomon was alive and enslaved somewhere along Bayou Boeuf in the vicinity of Marksville, Louisiana. Although that encompassed a large region with thousands of slaves, it was a start toward finding him.

To this day, several questions remain about the letter that Perry and Parker forwarded to Anne Northup. First, why didn't Solomon ask Bass to write to Anne to begin with instead of to the two white store owners? One possibility is that Solomon was afraid that Anne would come down to Louisiana to try to free him, which might have resulted in her being kidnapped into slavery, too.

Another puzzle is why didn't Bass mention in the letter that Edwin Epps owned Solomon? That would have made locating Solomon much easier. Perhaps Bass and Solomon were concerned that if Epps found out about the letter and saw that he was mentioned as owner of a kidnapped black man, he would sell Solomon rather than free him. Solomon might wind up in some remote place where rescuing him was impossible.

Finally, why didn't Anne write back informing her husband that she had gotten the letter and was trying to free him? Anne may have been afraid that her letter would be intercepted and shown to Solomon's owner, who would punish him for it.

Anne took the letter to the nearby village of Sandy Hill— now Hudson Falls—New York, and showed it to Henry B. Northup, the attorney whose family had once owned several of Solomon's ancestors and who had received the first letter. Henry B. looked into the matter and discovered "An Act to Protect the Free Citizens of this State from Being Kidnapped, or Reduced to Slavery." Henry B. Northup assembled documents proving that Solomon was a free black man. These included several affidavits—sworn written statements—from prominent citizens stating that Solomon had been free all his life until his kidnapping. Henry B. also asked Anne to write a memorial, or appeal, to Governor Washington Hunt verifying that Solomon

◆ "SOLOMON NORTHUP IS MY NAME!" ◆

was a free citizen of New York and describing their marriage, family, and what she knew about her husband's kidnapping. Anne's letter to Governor Hunt said in part:

> Your memorialist states that in 1841 she received information by a letter directed to Henry B. Northup, and postmarked at New Orleans, that Solomon had been kidnapped in Washington, put on board a vessel, and was then in New Orleans, but could not tell his destination.
>
> Your memorialist has been wholly unable to obtain information of where Solomon was, until September last, when another letter was received from Solomon, postmarked at Marksville, Louisiana, stating that he was held as a slave.
>
> The said Solomon is a free citizen of the State of New York, and is now wrongfully held in slavery, in or near Marksville, Louisiana.
>
> Anne Northup, November 19, 1852

In kidnapping cases the governor was expected to name an agent to handle the matter. On November 23, 1852, Governor Hunt appointed Henry B. Northup special agent in the Solomon Northup case. But Henry had trouble getting away because he was locked in a close election for a U.S. Congress seat that, fortunately for Solomon, he ultimately lost.

Not until December did Henry B. Northup pack his clothes, law books, and papers, and board a steamboat to begin the long journey to Marksville. Once there, he met with

Henry Bliss Northup, who traveled from New York to Louisiana to rescue Solomon, was a relative of the man who once owned Solomon's father.

longtime Marksville lawyer and state senator John P. Waddill. After studying Henry B. Northup's documents, Waddill agreed that Solomon had been wrongfully enslaved. He even offered to help Northup free Solomon. Pierre Soule, a U.S. senator from Marksville, also became deeply involved in the case and urged that Solomon be set free. The same was true of Louisiana politician Charles Magill Conrad, who had been United States secretary of war.

It may seem odd that these and other Louisiana lawmakers wholeheartedly agreed that Solomon had been wrongfully enslaved and should be allowed to return home to New York. Henry B. Northup was probably surprised by how agreeable they were. At this time Northerners and Southerners were arguing bitterly about slavery. Louisiana officials wanted to show the world—especially antislavery Northerners—that they were law-abiding and fair. In return they expected

Northerners to respect their right to own slaves, which was legal in the southern states.

But Solomon Northup couldn't be freed if he couldn't be found. Where was he? The letter to the two store owners revealed that Solomon lived near Marksville along Bayou Boeuf. That was a start, but neither John P. Waddill nor anyone else in Marksville knew of any slave in the area named Solomon Northup.

Having delayed coming to Louisiana because of the election, Henry B. Northup was determined to make up for lost time by going to great lengths to find Solomon. He made plans to visit every plantation along Bayou Boeuf one at a time.

Northup asked Waddill a question that had been puzzling him. Did he know anyone in or near Marksville who hated slavery enough to have written and mailed the letter for Solomon? Waddill said he knew just such a man: "He is a generous, inoffensive man, but always maintaining the wrong side of an argument. He is a carpenter. His name is Bass."

Suddenly Waddill had an idea. He asked to see the letter to the two store owners once more and studied the top where it said "Bayou Boeuf, August 15, 1852." The Marksville attorney asked an assistant in his law office if he knew where Samuel Bass had worked during the past summer. "Somewhere on Bayou Boeuf" was the answer.

"He is the man who can tell us about Solomon Northup!" Waddill declared.

Henry B. Northup hired a carriage, and on New Year's Day of 1853 he traveled a few miles to a settlement on the Red River where Samuel Bass was working. He found Bass, who agreed to speak with him privately. When the visitor introduced himself as Henry B. Northup from New York, Bass could hardly contain his joy, for that name had often been mentioned to him as an acquaintance of Solomon's.

"Mr. Bass," said the lawyer from New York, "allow me to ask if you were on Bayou Boeuf last August."

"Yes, sir, I was there," Bass admitted.

"Did you write a letter for a colored man to some gentlemen in Saratoga Springs?" continued Henry B. Northup.

Bass wasn't ready to reveal that information until he knew a little more about the visitor. "Excuse me, sir, if I say that is none of your business!"

Mr. Northup then explained that he had come all the way from New York to free a black man named Solomon Northup who had been kidnapped into slavery. A letter dated August 15 and postmarked at Marksville, Louisiana, had drawn him to this area.

Convinced that Henry B. Northup was telling the truth, Samuel Bass told him everything he wanted to know. "I am the man who wrote the letter. If you have come to rescue Solomon Northup, I am glad to see you."

"When did you last see him, and where is he?" Mr. Northup asked.

"I last saw him Christmas—a week ago today," Bass answered. The carpenter then revealed the information that Henry B. Northup had traveled 1,500 miles to hear. "He is the slave of Edwin Epps, a planter on Bayou Boeuf, near Holmesville. He is not known as Solomon Northup. He is called Platt." Samuel Bass even drew a map for Henry B. Northup showing Epps's plantation and the roads by which it could be reached.

Edwin Epps could be expected to fight to keep a valuable property like Solomon Northup from being taken from him. To prevent that, and to make absolutely certain that Solomon had been wrongfully enslaved, the local sheriff accompanied Henry B. Northup to the Epps plantation. They arrived by carriage on the cold morning of January 3, 1853—just after Epps went inside to get his whip.

Solomon watched as the two white men approached through the cotton field. Like the other shivering slaves, he wondered who the two visitors were.

Identifying himself as the sheriff, one of the white men asked, "Where's the boy they call Platt?"

Solomon stepped forward, and the sheriff began questioning him. "Have you any other name than Platt?"

"Solomon Northup is my name!" he answered.

What was his wife's name? Where had their marriage taken place? How many children did they have and what were their names?

Solomon answered the sheriff's questions correctly. "Do you know that man?" asked the sheriff, pointing to his companion in the tall hat and suit.

Although the gentleman looked vaguely familiar, Solomon couldn't identify him at first. Then suddenly he knew. "Henry B. Northup! Thank God! Thank God!" Solomon was so excited that he could not say another word for quite a while. Bursting into tears, he clasped Henry B. by both hands and wouldn't let go.

"Sol," said his old acquaintance from New York, "throw down that sack. Your cotton-picking days are over. Come with us to the man you live with."

As they walked toward the Epps house, Solomon suddenly felt faint and had to be held up by the sheriff and Mr. Northup. Epps met the three men outside his home and invited them inside. When he learned that he was about to lose a slave for whom he had paid $1,500, he went into a rage.

"You damned nigger!" Epps yelled. "Why did you not tell me you were free when I bought you?"

"Master Epps," Solomon answered, "you did not take the trouble to ask me. Besides, I told one of my owners that I was free—and was whipped almost to death for it." Solomon later said that he would have given Epps a "parting kick"—if it wouldn't have jeopardized his rescue from bondage.

Epps then demanded that Solomon name the man who had mailed the letter at Marksville for him, but he refused. As Epps cursed and threatened to kill both Solomon and whoever had helped him, Henry B. Northup and the sheriff said it was time to depart.

Edwin Epps wasn't about to give Solomon up without a legal struggle, though. He ordered his slave Bob to saddle his horse, then off Epps galloped to the office of H. Taylor, his lawyer, to see if anything could be done to keep him from losing Platt. Meanwhile, with Epps gone and Solomon preparing to leave with the sheriff and Henry B. Northup, Solomon's fellow slaves in the cotton field came up to him to say farewell.

Phebe went first, whispering in his ear, "Wish I could go, too, Platt." Old Abram and Bob also came to say goodbye. So did Mrs. Epps, who remarked that now there was no one to play the violin for her. But the person who was moved the most by Solomon's departure was Patsey, who threw her arms around his neck and said: "You're goin' way off yonder, where we'll never see you anymore! You saved me a good many whippins, Platt. I'm glad you're goin' to be free. But, oh, God! What will become of me?"

Solomon boarded the carriage with the sheriff and Northup. With a crack of the driver's whip, off they went. They were pulling out of the Epps plantation when Solomon glanced back and saw Patsey watching forlornly with the others. He waved at them, but just then the carriage rounded a bend and they were gone from his view forever.

Solomon hoped to head back to New York immediately, but Henry B. explained that one more hurdle remained. The next day there was to be a big legal meeting in Marksville, at which Solomon would be officially freed from bondage. It was just a formality, Henry B. explained. But despite the reassur-ances, Solomon knew that Epps was determined to keep him as a slave. Until he actually stood on free soil, Solomon couldn't rest easy.

The following morning, January 4, 1853, Solomon attended the legal meeting. Participants included a judge, the sheriff, Henry B. Northup, John P. Waddill, and Epps and his lawyer, H. Taylor.

Everything went as smoothly as Henry B. Northup had promised. Henry B. presented some legal papers. The sheriff related his conversation with Solomon in the cotton field, and then questioned him further. Finally, Lawyer Taylor explained that he had studied the case extensively and had concluded that Epps should sign a paper acknowledging that Solomon was entitled to his freedom. The moment Edwin Epps signed his name to the document, Solomon Northup was free after 12 years of bondage.

Once the meeting ended the two Northups began the long trip home. They hurried to the landing along the Red River and boarded a steamboat that took them to New Orleans. While there, Henry B. Northup wanted to meet Theophilus Freeman, the slave dealer in whose pen Solomon had been held. Henry hoped to determine whether Freeman should be prosecuted for knowingly selling a free black man. The two Northups entered the very room where William Ford had purchased Solomon 12 years earlier. They soon gave up the idea of prosecuting Freeman, however. He no longer owned the slave pen, and when seen on the streets of New Orleans, he struck Solomon as "a low, miserable, broken-down man."

After two days in New Orleans the two Northups headed north by railroad and steamboat. They made their way up the East Coast through the Carolinas and Virginia, and on January 17, 1853, after nearly two weeks of travel, they arrived in Washington, D.C. Henry B. Northup insisted that they spend a few days in the nation's capital because he felt that James Birch should be punished for knowingly buying a free black man from Merrill Brown and Abram Hamilton and then selling him as a slave. Birch still lived in Washington, D.C., and Henry B. Northup had no trouble getting him arrested and quickly brought to trial. Proving Birch's guilt was another matter. He denied knowing that Solomon was a free man and had several friends testify on his behalf. Solomon wasn't allowed to present evidence against Birch because at that time black people weren't permitted to testify against whites in the courts of our nation's capital. Despite being under oath to tell the truth, Birch concocted an outrageous story. Instead of being the victim, Birch claimed, Solomon was the guilty party. He had pretended to be a slave so that he and his two partners in crime, Merrill Brown and Abram Hamilton, could make a fortune. In other words, Solomon had been part of a scheme to sell himself into slavery!

Since Solomon was not allowed to refute this lie, the judge didn't know what to think. He ruled that there was not enough evidence to convict Birch of buying and selling a man he knew to be free. James Birch was found not guilty of all charges and released from custody.

Despite feeling bitter disappointment at the verdict, Solomon was grateful that Birch's trial had at least been quick. After just three days in Washington, D.C., the Northups resumed their journey on January 20. As they continued northward by train and carriage, Solomon's heart beat faster with each passing mile. Soon he would be with his family!

On Sunday morning, January 23, 1853, Solomon knocked on the front door of a cottage in Glens Falls, New York. A young woman with a little boy at her side answered the door. For a few seconds they stared at each other, the man thinking he was at the wrong house, the young woman wondering whether she had opened her door to a stranger. Then Solomon realized that the woman was his younger daughter, Margaret, who had been just seven years old when he had last seen her. At the same time Margaret realized that this vaguely familiar middle-age man was her long-lost father.

Moments later Solomon's older daughter, Elizabeth, entered the room. Close at her heels was Solomon's wife, Anne.

"They embraced me," Solomon later recalled, "and with

tears flowing down their cheeks, hung upon my neck. When
our emotions subsided, the household gathered round the fire.
We conversed of the thousands of events that had occurred—
the hopes and fears, the joys and sorrows, the trials and
troubles we had each experienced during the long separation."

Solomon was saddened to learn that his mother had died
in his absence. His son, Alonzo, was well, but was in the western part of New York raising funds to buy his father
out of slavery if nothing else worked. The young boy at
Margaret's side was Solomon Northup Staunton, named for
the grandfather he had never before seen.

People in and around Glens Falls, Saratoga Springs, and
Sandy Hill, New York, were familiar with Solomon's story and
were eager to see him. A huge reception in Solomon's honor was
held at Sandy Hill just a day after his arrival. One of the event's
organizers was David Wilson, a lawyer and former superinten-
dent of area schools who also wrote books on local history.

Speaking privately to Solomon, Wilson confided to him
his belief that the public would enjoy reading about his experiences in slavery. Solomon accepted Wilson's offer to help him
write his autobiography. Solomon wrote a description of his
life as a slave; Wilson transformed the raw notes into a book.

Working furiously, the two men completed Solomon's
336-page autobiography in only three months. The book was
published that July by Derby & Miller, a firm based in Auburn,
New York. It was given the cumbersome title *Twelve Years a
Slave: Narrative of Solomon Northup, a Citizen of New-York, Kidnapped in Washington City in 1841, and Rescued in 1853, From a
Cotton Plantation Near the Red River, in Louisiana.*

Twelve Years a Slave was a rousing success. Reviewers lavished praise upon Solomon's book. For example, the *Syracuse Journal* called it "one of the most effective books against slavery that was ever written." The *New York Tribune* declared, "No one can contemplate [the book] without a new conviction of the hideousness of [slavery]." The *New York Evangelist* boldly predicted that *Twelve Years a Slave* would increase the "anti-slavery sentiment of the country."

The glowing reviews boosted the book's sales. It sold 8,000 copies the first month, which was quite a start. By 1856, when publication of Solomon's original book came to a halt, it had sold more than 30,000 copies. That was a big number for the 1850s and would be an excellent total for a nonfiction book even today.

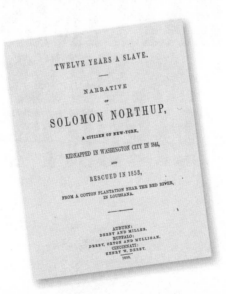

The first edition of TWELVE YEARS A SLAVE *was published in 1853.*

CHAPTER 10

"I HAD BEEN RESTORED TO HAPPINESS AND LIBERTY"

AMONG THE READERS OF *TWELVE YEARS A SLAVE* was a judge from Fonda, New York, 50 miles from Solomon's home in Glens Falls. His name was Thaddeus St. John. When Judge St. John read how Merrill Brown and Abram Hamilton sold Solomon into slavery in Washington, D.C., in 1841, he was reminded of an experience of his own at that very time.

While stopping in Baltimore during a trip to Washington, D.C., St. John had run into two acquaintances from New York State—Alexander Merrill and Joseph Russell—who were accompanied by a black man. "What are you doing here, Joe?" St. John asked Russell. Seemingly upset about being recognized, Russell and Merrill rushed up to St. John and requested that he not call them by their real names.

Judge St. John considered that mighty odd. Merrill and Russell soon displayed even more bizarre behavior. On the eve of President William Henry Harrison's funeral procession, St. John met the same three men at Gadsby's Hotel in Washington, D.C. He wasn't sure what the black man was doing with them, but his impression was that he was not a slave. Then on his return trip to New York, St. John once again ran into Merrill and Russell, in Baltimore. This time the black man was not with them. Apparently having suddenly struck it rich, Merrill and Russell sported expensive new clothing along with gold watches and fancy canes. St. John, half-kidding, accused them of selling their black companion and remarked that they must have gotten $500 for him. To the judge's surprise Merrill bragged that they had sold him for $150 more than that.

Judge St. John assumed they were joking, for selling a free black man—as their companion had appeared to be—was a serious crime. When St. John questioned them further, the two white men said that they were just pulling his leg. They had actually made a fortune—or so they claimed—by gambling with several southern gentlemen.

Reading about how the two "circus men" had sold Solomon Northup, Thaddeus St. John began to think that his two acquaintances were the guilty parties. After finishing *Twelve Years a Slave*, St. John wrote to Solomon and arranged to meet him in Fonda.

Despite the passage of time Thaddeus St. John and Solomon Northup recognized one another instantly. Solomon was the black man St. John had seen with Alexander Merrill and Joseph Russell. Evidently St. John's two acquaintances really had sold Solomon Northup into slavery.

Solomon contacted Henry B. Northup and informed him that he had discovered the true identities of the two men who had lured him to Washington, D.C., and then sold him to Birch. Doing a little detective work, the two Northups learned that Alexander Merrill, alias Merrill Brown, was from Gloversville, New York, just 30 miles from where Solomon and his family had lived in Saratoga Springs. On the Fourth of July, 1854, Alexander Merrill visited Gloversville to enjoy the holiday festivities at his parents' home. The two Northups aided the police in seizing Merrill, as described a few days later in the *Albany Evening Journal:*

Henry B. Northup has spent a great deal of time and
money ferreting out the scoundrel, and they have no doubt
got the man. Solomon identifies him without a doubt. Merrill
has long been regarded as a desperate fellow. They found him
asleep, with a heavy bowie knife and a brace of pistols on the
floor by his side.

Bulletins circulated alerting police to be on the lookout for
Joseph Russell, alias Abram Hamilton, the other man wanted for
selling Solomon Northup into slavery. Shortly after Merrill was
captured, two police officers found Russell working as a boat
captain on New York's Erie Canal. They arrested Russell, who
along with his partner Merrill was jailed in a town a few miles
from Saratoga Springs. Pending their trial, Russell and Merrill
were each released on $5,000 bail, equal today to about $125,000.

Russell and Merrill's trial for kidnapping and enslaving
Solomon Northup opened in February 1855. The courtroom
was packed, for Solomon's book had made the case famous.
As part of Russell and Merrill's defense, slave dealer James
Birch sent a statement to the court from Washington, D.C.
It repeated Birch's lie from his own trial that Solomon had
been part of a scheme to sell himself into slavery. Birch added
an extra touch this time, saying that Solomon wanted to be
enslaved so badly that he played on a borrowed fiddle in the
Washington, D.C., slave pen to prove his value.

Countering Birch's story was Thaddeus St. John, who
testified that he had seen Solomon with Russell and Merrill in
Washington, D.C. St. John also repeated what Merrill had told
him in Baltimore, that he and Russell had sold Solomon for $650.

Once again, enough doubt was cast on what had occurred that the defendants avoided a guilty verdict. Merrill and Russell, like Birch, were never punished for their crimes against Solomon Northup. Yet, despite not seeing justice done in his case, Solomon had regained what he treasured most: his freedom and his family.

Solomon received a $3,000 payment for the publication of his book—equal to around $75,000 today. He spent some of the money on a piece of land in Glens Falls next to the cottage where his married daughter Margaret lived with her husband and their child. Evidently Solomon planned to build a home for Anne and himself on the property, but he never did. Instead, he and Anne remained in Margaret's house. To earn a living, Solomon worked as a carpenter. From time to time he also went on the road giving talks about his 12 years as a slave.

Samuel Bass had once told Solomon, "If I can succeed in getting you away from here, it will be a good act that I shall like to think of all of my life." Had he lived a little longer, Bass might have visited Solomon and his family. But the man who had done so much to rescue Solomon from slavery became ill with pneumonia just a few months after Solomon's return to New York State. In the summer of 1853, while still in Louisiana, Samuel Bass died at the age of only about 48. It is unknown whether Edwin Epps ever discovered that Bass sent the letters that helped free Solomon.

Around 1860, when he was in his early 50s, Solomon Northup disappeared from view. "We simply don't know what became of him," explains Renee Moore, who in 1999 founded an annual event in Saratoga Springs called Solomon Northup Day—A Celebration of Freedom. "He may have died of natural causes somewhere. Another guess is that he may have been killed by his abductors as he traveled about speaking about his ordeal and his autobiography. Thus far, his final resting place has not been determined."

These few words by Solomon at the end of *Twelve Years a Slave* regarding his return home are a fitting memorial to him:

> *My heart overflowed as I looked upon old familiar scenes, and found myself in the midst of friends of other days . . . I had been restored to happiness and liberty."*

AFTERWORD

SOLOMON NORTHUP
BORN 1808 A FREE MAN. LURED
FROM SARATOGA, KIDNAPPED &
SOLD INTO SLAVERY, 1841;
RESCUED, 1853. AUTHOR,
"TWELVE YEARS A SLAVE".
CITY OF SARATOGA SPRINGS 1999

FROM 1780 TO THE EARLY 1860s LARGE NUMBERS OF slaves won their freedom, becoming known as free blacks or free persons of color. Escaping to the northern states and Canada was the most common way that slaves achieved their liberty. At least 50,000 slaves escaped by following the North Star to freedom.

Strange but true, another way that slaves won their freedom was by buying themselves. Slaves typically had one day of the week off—Sunday. By running errands and doing other tasks on Sundays, slaves were paid nickels and dimes in tips. After decades of earning small change, some slaves saved enough "Sunday money" to purchase and free themselves.

Often as their own lives drew to a close, slaveholders realized that slavery was evil. Some wrote out wills that would free their slaves as of a certain date. For example, according to George Washington's will his slaves were to be set free after he and his wife, Martha, died.

While it is well known that many African Americans went from slavery to freedom, it is less known that thousands of black people went from freedom to slavery, mainly by being kidnapped like Solomon Northup. How many thousands suffered this fate is unknown because no records were kept chronicling all the free blacks who were enslaved.

The laws in the South actually encouraged the enslavement of free black people. One of the rules of law in the U.S. is that a person is presumed innocent until proven guilty. But in the South in slavery days, black people walking along a road or

Every year, on the third Saturday in July—the week of Solomon's birthday—the city of Saratoga Springs celebrates Solomon Northup Day. Above is a photo of Northup's descendants taken in 1999 after the mayor presented a historical marker to the city.

through a town were presumed to be runaway slaves and were arrested and jailed. The burden was upon them to prove that they were free.

To make things worse, in most of the South, African Americans who were jailed for any reason whatsoever were required to pay their jail and court costs. Those who lacked the money could be sold into bondage to pay the bills. The result was the enslavement of many free black people.

Another unjust law that was widespread in both the South and the North barred free black people from testifying in court. This meant that they had to sit silently at trials while fake evidence was brought forth identifying them as slaves.

Of course, slavery of any kind is evil. But famed African-American leader Frederick Douglass, himself a runaway slave, felt that there was something especially awful about the enslavement of free people like Solomon Northup. In 1853 Douglass wrote about Solomon: "Think of it! For thirty years a man, with all a man's hopes, fears, and aspirations—with a wife and children to call him husband and father—with a home, humble it may be. Then for twelve years a thing, classed with mules and horses, torn from his home and family, and driven to toil in a cotton field, by the lash of an inhuman master. Oh! It is horrible. It chills the blood."

The enslavement of free blacks lasted until 1865, the year slavery was abolished in the United States by the North's victory in the Civil War. Then all the remaining Solomon Northups—and all the other slaves like Patsey, Old Abram, Wiley, and Eliza and her children—were forever released from bondage.

TIME LINE

SLAVERY IN THE UNITED STATES BEFORE, DURING, AND AFTER THE LIFE OF SOLOMON NORTHUP

1619 Dutch traders bring 20 African slaves to the British colony of James-town, Virginia. Spanish settlers had been capturing and importing slaves from Africa to the Americas, including the present-day United States, since the early 1500s. These early slaves were treated like indentured servants and freed after a set period of servitude.

1640 A runaway black servant named John Punch is sentenced to a lifetime of enslavement, becoming one of the first African-American slaves for life in the American colonies.

1641 Massachusetts becomes the first colony to legalize slavery. Other colonies soon begin to recognize slavery as a legal institution.

1654 In Virginia, blacks are allowed to own slaves. Anthony Johnson becomes the first black man to hold slaves for life.

1662 Virginia enacts a law dictating that children of black mothers shall assume the social status of the mother: Children of free mothers shall be free, and children of enslaved mothers shall be slaves. Other southern colonies quickly follow suit, but northern colonies never pass specific laws regarding hereditary slavery.

1775 In April, the American Revolutionary War begins with the Battles of Lexington and Concord. The world's first abolitionist society (a group organized to oppose slavery) is founded in Philadelphia.

1776 On July 4 in Philadelphia, members of the Continental Congress sign the Declaration of Independence to create the United States of America. The Declaration states, "All men are created equal."

1777 Vermont becomes the first U.S. territory to abolish slavery.

1780 Pennsylvania becomes the first U.S. state to abolish slavery.

1790 The results of the first United States census show that of the population of 3.9 million, nearly 700,000 (18 percent) are slaves.

1793 Congress passes the first federal Fugitive Slave Law, which allows slaveholders to pursue runaways across state lines. Later versions impose harsh penalties on those who harbor runaway slaves.

1808 Solomon Northup is born a free man in Minerva, New York. In the same year, the United States outlaws the importing of African slaves. Solomon probably came in contact with black slaves while growing up in New York.

1820 The Missouri Compromise admits Missouri into the Union and forbids slavery in any new western territories north of parallel 36°30'.

1827 Slavery is abolished in Solomon's home state of New York.

1829 Solomon marries Anne Hampton on Christmas Day.

1840 On May 14, New York State passes a law making it the state's duty to locate and recover any New York resident kidnapped and sold into slavery.

1841 Solomon is kidnapped and sold into slavery in Washington, D.C., transported to New Orleans, Louisiana, and sold again.

1843 On April 9, Solomon is sold to Edwin Epps.

1846 New Jersey becomes the last northern state to completely abolish slavery. The Border States of Maryland, Missouri, and West Virginia allow slavery until the Civil War; the remaining slaves in Kentucky and Delaware are not freed until the passage of the 13th Amendment to the Constitution in 1865.

1850 The Compromise of 1850 passes in September. It admits California into the Union as a free state and continues slavery in Washington, D.C., though it bans buying and selling slaves there.

1852 Harriet Beecher Stowe's antislavery book *Uncle Tom's Cabin* is published. It becomes the second-best-selling book in the country behind the Bible.

1852 Samuel Bass mails Solomon's letter to Saratoga Springs, New York, on August 15.

1853 On January 4, Solomon is freed. His autobiography, *Twelve Years a Slave*, is published later in the year.

1861 The Civil War officially begins with the Battle of Fort Sumter in April.

1862 Slavery is officially abolished in Washington, D.C., when President Lincoln signs the Compensated Emancipation Act on April 16.

1863 On New Year's Day, President Abraham Lincoln issues the Emancipation Proclamation, freeing all slaves in the states of the Confederacy. Because Lincoln did not have control over the Confederacy, the Emancipation Proclamation didn't actually free any southern slaves. Ironically, the Proclamation did not apply to Union border states.

1865 The Civil War ends on April 9; President Lincoln is assassinated on April 14. On December 6, the 13th Amendment to the Constitution is ratified by the states, officially abolishing slavery in the United States.

1860s Solomon Northup disappears from public view. The exact date and cause of his death are unknown.

BIBLIOGRAPHY

BOOKS

Brode, Patrick. *The Odyssey of John Anderson.* Toronto: University of Toronto Press, 1989.

Brown, John. *Slave Life in Georgia.* Savannah, Georgia: The Beehive Press, 1996 (reprint of 1855 edition).

Northup, Solomon. *Twelve Years a Slave.* Baton Rouge, Louisiana: State University Press, 1996 (reprint of 1853 edition).

Ploski, Harry A., and Roscoe C. Brown, Jr., editors. *The Negro Almanac.* New York: Bellwether Publishing Company, 1967.

NEWSPAPERS

New York Times, January 20, 1853
Albany Evening Journal, July 9, 1854
Saratoga Whig, July 14, 1854
The Liberator, August 26, 1853

INTERVIEW

Renee Moore, Founder of Solomon Northup Day—
A Celebration of Freedom, Saratoga Springs, New York
(interviewed in late 2010 and early 2011)

ONLINE RESOURCES

For information about Solomon Northup and Solomon Northup Day, held annually in Saratoga Springs, New York, go to http://www.americaslibrary.gov/es/ny/es_ny_slave_1.html and http://saratoganygenweb.com/images/snorthupday06.htm.

Solomon Northup's Odyssey (1984), a Gordon Parks TV drama starring Avery Brooks, is based on Solomon's life and is available at http://www.imdb.com/title/tt0088148/.

Solomon and Anne moved into the Old Fort House after their marriage in 1829. It is now a museum and offers historical education programs on Solomon Northup. For more information, visit http://www.fedward.com/history/oldfort/oldfort.htm.

The Library of Congress in Washington, D.C., has an exhibition called "The African American Odyssey: A Quest for Full Citizenship." Read through their resources at: http://memory.loc.gov/ammem/aaohtml/exhibit/aointro.html.

The National Underground Railroad Freedom Center in Cincinnati, Ohio, is a museum that has exhibits on slavery from the time of the Underground Railroad to today. Resources are available at http://www.freedomcenter.org/. The center has an app available for free on the Apple iTunes store.

INDEX

Illustrations are indicated by **boldface** type.

A

Abolitionists **73,** 74, 112

B

Baltimore, Md. 19, 103, 105
Bass, Samuel 71–86, 89, 90,
    93–94, 106, 114
Bayou Boeuf, La.: plantations
    55, 57, 61, 72, 86, 93, 94
Bayou Huff Power, La. 50, 55
Birch, James
    purchase of Solomon Nor-
        thup 10, 21, 24, 32, 104
    as slave trader 9–10, 13,
        21–22, 31
    trial 98–99, 106

C

Chafin, Anderson 36–39,
    41–42
Civil War 5, 111, 113, 114
Conrad, Charles Magill 92
Cotton presses 42, **43**

D

Douglass, Frederick 111

E

Emancipation Proclamation
    114
Epps, Edwin
    as cotton planter 50–69,
        86–87, 94–97
    house 71, 72, 74, 75, **76**
    purchase of Solomon Nor-
        thup 47, 72, 113
Epps, Mary 54–55, 63, 67, 68,
    69

F

Ford, William 25, 32–42,
    45–47, 98
Freeman, Theophilus 31–34,
    98

G

Gadsby's Hotel, Washington,
    D.C. 19, 20, 103
Garrison, William Lloyd **73**
Great Crocodile Swamp, La.
    44

H

Harrison, William Henry 20,
    103
Harvesting
    cotton **52**
    sugarcane 61, **62**

Illustration Credits

Cover (hands), Mark Thiessen, NGS Staff; cover (field), biletskiy/Shutterstock; 2, Mark Thiessen, NGS Staff; 8, The Bridgeman Art Library; 11, Corbis; 12, Library of Congress; 14, Alexander Demyanenko/Shutterstock; 17, Library of Congress; 19, National Geographic Maps; 23, Bettmann/ Corbis; 25, National Geographic Maps; 30, Andrey Orlov/Shutterstock; 33, Courtesy the Sue L. Eakin Estate; 35, Judith B. Fradin; 40, Sergej Razvodovskij/Shutterstock; 43, Kean Collection/Getty Images; 45, National Geographic Maps; 48, VLDR/Shutterstock; 52, Bettmann/Corbis; 56, James T. Tanner/Tensas River National Wildlife Refuge, U.S. Fish and Wildlife Service, Ivory-Billed Woodpecker Records (Mss. 4171), Louisiana and Lower Mississippi Valley Collections, Louisiana State University Libraries, Baton Rouge, Louisiana, U.S.A.; 61, Stargazer/Shutterstock; 62, Library of Congress; 63, Oliver McPherson Collection/Louisiana State University Libraries; 70, Mostovyi Sergii Igorevich/Shutterstock; 73, Bettmann/Corbis; 76, The Epps House, Louisiana State University at Alexandria. Used with Permission, 2011; 82, Russell Shively/Shutterstock; 88, Courtesy Northwestern University Special Collections; 92, Courtesy the Sue L. Eakin Estate; 101, Courtesy the Sue L. Eakin Estate; 102, Ingvar Bjork/Shutterstock; 108, Johnnie Roberts/Program Coordinator/Heritage Area Visitor Center; 110, Courtesy Renee Moore.

The National Geographic Society is one of the world's largest nonprofit scientific and educational organizations. Founded in 1888 to "increase and diffuse geographic knowledge," the Society works to inspire people to care about the planet. National Geographic reflects the world through its magazines, television programs, films, music and radio, books, DVDs, maps, exhibitions, live events, school publishing programs, interactive media and merchandise. *National Geographic* magazine, the Society's official journal, published in English and 33 local-language editions, is read by more than 38 million people each month. The National Geographic Channel reaches 320 million households in 34 languages in 166 countries. National Geographic Digital Media receives more than 15 million visitors a month. National Geographic has funded more than 9,400 scientific research, conservation and exploration projects and supports an education program promoting geography literacy. For more information, visit nationalgeographic.com.

For more information, please call 1-800-NGS LINE (647-5463) or write to the following address:

National Geographic Society
1145 17th Street N.W.
Washington, D.C. 20036-4688 U.S.A.

Visit us online at www.nationalgeographic.com/books

For librarians and teachers: www.ngchildrensbooks.org

More for kids from National Geographic: kids.nationalgeographic.com

For information about special discounts for bulk purchases, please contact National Geographic Books Special Sales: ngspecsales@ngs.org

For rights or permissions inquiries, please contact National Geographic Books Subsidiary Rights: ngbookrights@ngs.org